# LORETO TRAVEL GUIDE 2024

Your Essential Handbook to Sightseeing, History, Food, and Culture.

## ROBERT BROWN

Copyright © 2024 by Robert Brown

All rights reserved. No part of this publication may be reproduced, distributed, or transmitted in any form or by any means, including photocopying, recording, or other electronic or mechanical methods, without the prior written permission of the publisher.

# Table of Content

| | |
|---|---|
| Table of Content | 2 |
| Introduction to Loreto: Why You Should Visit Loreto in 2024. | 5 |
| Brief History of Loreto | 7 |
| Overview of Loreto's Culture and Heritage | 9 |
| Chapter 1: Planning Your Trip | 13 |
|     Best Time to Visit Loreto | 13 |
|     Visa Requirements and Travel Documents | 16 |
|     Packing Tips for Your Loreto Adventure | 18 |
| Chapter 2: Getting to Loreto | 22 |
|     Transportation Options (Air, Road, Sea) | 22 |
|     Airport Information and Ground Transportation | 24 |
|     Border Crossing Information | 27 |
| Chapter 3: Accommodation | 31 |
|     Luxury Resorts and Hotels | 31 |
|     BudgetFriendly Accommodations | 33 |
|     EcoFriendly Lodging Options | 36 |
| Chapter 4: Exploring Loreto | 39 |
|     Top Attractions and Landmarks | 39 |
|     Hidden Gems Off the Beaten Path | 42 |
|     Guided Tours and Excursions | 44 |
| Chapter 5: Outdoor Adventures | 48 |
| Snorkeling and Diving Spots | 48 |

| | |
|---|---|
| Hiking Trails and Nature Reserves | 51 |
| Fishing Charters and Water Sports | 54 |
| Chapter 6: Immersing Yourself in Culture | 57 |
| Museums and Art Galleries | 57 |
| Traditional Festivals and Events | 60 |
| Interaction with Local Communities | 64 |
| Chapter 7: Dining and Nightlife | 67 |
| Restaurants Serving Authentic Cuisine | 67 |
| Bars and Nightclubs for Evening Entertainment | 70 |
| Street Food and Culinary Experiences | 73 |
| Chapter 8: Shopping in Loreto | 77 |
| Local Markets and Souvenir Shops | 77 |
| Handcrafted Goods and Artisanal Products | 80 |
| Sustainable Shopping Options | 83 |
| Chapter 9: Practical Information | 87 |
| Currency and Payment Methods | 87 |
| Currency: | 87 |
| Accepted Payment Methods: | 87 |
| Currency Exchange: | 89 |
| Tips for Handling Money: | 89 |
| Language Spoken in Loreto | 90 |
| Emergency Contact Numbers | 91 |
| Chapter 10: Responsible Travel Practices | 94 |
| Environmental Conservation Efforts | 94 |
| Respectful Interaction with Local Culture | 97 |
| Minimizing Your Ecological Footprint | 100 |
| Glossary of Loreto Related Terms | 104 |
| Conclusion and Departure Tips | 108 |

| To End With | 108 |
|---|---|
| Departure Tips: | 108 |

# Introduction to Loreto: Why You Should Visit Loreto in 2024.

Nestled along the gorgeous coast of the Sea of Cortez in Baja California Sur, Loreto beckons guests with its timeless charm and natural beauty. As you examine your travel plans for 2024, consider embarking on a memorable adventure to this hidden jewel of Mexico.

Why Visit Loreto in 2024?

1. **Preservation of Natural Wonders:** In an everevolving world, Loreto serves as a sanctuary for environment aficionados. Immerse yourself in the stunning scenery of the Sierra de la Giganta mountain range, explore the marine richness of the protected marine park, or simply unwind on pristine beaches kissed by the azure waves of the Sea of Cortez.

2. **Cultural Richness and Heritage:** Beyond its natural attractiveness, Loreto features a rich collection of history and culture begging to be discovered. Delve into the town's colonial past by meandering through its

cobblestone alleys studded with centuries-old buildings, or immerse yourself in the rich customs of local communities through festivals and cultural activities.

3. **Sustainable Tourism Initiatives:** In an era where environmental protection is vital, Loreto stands at the forefront of sustainable tourism practices. Experience the region's commitment to eco-friendly projects, from ethical wildlife interactions to community-driven conservation efforts aimed at conserving the region's delicate ecosystems for years to come.

4. **Authentic Culinary Experiences:** Indulge your senses in the flavors of Baja cuisine as you savor fresh fish specialties and traditional dishes prepared from locally sourced ingredients. From beachside palapa restaurants to beautiful cafes situated away in historic plazas, Loreto provides a culinary excursion that will excite your taste buds and leave you demanding more.

5. **Off-the-Beaten-Path Adventures:** Escape the throng and engage in off-the-beaten-path activities that uncover the true character of Loreto. Whether you're seeking isolation amidst rough desert scenery, seeking adrenaline-pumping water activities, or seeking cultural immersion in remote settlements, Loreto provides a range of experiences that cater to any traveler's desires.

As you examine your vacation plans for 2024, consider Loreto as your next location. Whether you want adventure, relaxation, or cultural enrichment, Loreto guarantees an extraordinary vacation that will leave a lasting mark on your heart and spirit.

# Brief History of Loreto

1. **Ancient Origins:** Loreto's history extends back to ancient times when indigenous tribes, like the Cochimí, occupied the region. These early settlers thrived in harmony with the difficult desert nature, leaving behind remnants of their existence in the form of cave paintings and archaeological sites dispersed throughout the area.

2. **Spanish Colonization:** In 1697, Spanish missionaries led by Jesuit priest Juan María de Salvatierra established the Mission of Our Lady of Loreto, marking the beginning of Spanish colonization in the region. The mission functioned as a vital hub for the development of Christianity and European influence in the Baja California peninsula, providing the foundation for the town of Loreto to prosper as the first capital of the Californias.

3. **Colonial Era**: Throughout the colonial era, Loreto thrived as a dynamic colonial outpost, functioning as the political, religious, and economic hub of the province. The town became a strategic harbour for Spanish galleons going between Mexico and the Philippines, contributing to its economy and cultural prominence.

4. **Decline and Revival**: In the late 18th century, Loreto's significance decreased following the expulsion of the Jesuits and the move of the capital to La Paz. However, the town witnessed a renaissance in the 20th century with the growth of tourism and fishing businesses, attracting visitors lured to its clean beaches, rich marine life, and historical beauty.

5. **Modern Loreto:** Today, Loreto continues to amaze visitors with its blend of colonial heritage, natural beauty, and real Mexican culture. The town's historic core contains wellpreserved colonial buildings, notably the landmark Mission of Our Lady of Loreto, a tribute to its long reputation as the cradle of California civilization.

6. **UNESCO World Heritage Recognition:** In acknowledgment of its historic value, the Mission of Our Lady of Loreto, along with other Jesuit missions in Baja California, was designated a UNESCO World Heritage Site in 1993, thus solidifying Loreto's position in history

as a treasure trove of colonial architecture and religious art.

7. **Preserving the Past, Embracing the Future**: As Loreto continues to flourish as a renowned destination for ecotourism and sustainable travel, efforts to conserve its rich cultural history and natural landscapes remain vital. Visitors to Loreto are welcome to explore its historic past, immerse themselves in its lively present, and embark on a journey of discovery that celebrates the ageless allure of this coastal gem.

# Overview of Loreto's Culture and Heritage

Loreto, a charming town tucked on the eastern coast of the Baja California Peninsula, is a cultural and historical treasure trove waiting to be explored. Rich in customs, culture, and colonial heritage, Loreto provides tourists a glimpse into its dynamic past and present.

1. **Colonial Architecture**: At the heart of Loreto is its historic downtown, where narrow cobblestone lanes thread their way past colonialera buildings adorned with

colorful facades and beautiful wroughtiron balconies. The crown gem of Loreto's architectural history is the Mission of Our Lady of Loreto, a superb example of Spanish colonial architecture dating back to the 17th century. Visitors can marvel at its Baroquestyle exterior, covered with magnificent sculptures and religious imagery, and explore its well preserved interior, with a breathtaking altar and intricately carved wooden furnishings.

2. **Religious Festivals and Traditions:** Throughout the year, Loreto comes alive with religious festivals and cultural events that pay homage to its Catholic tradition and indigenous roots. The Feast of Our Lady of Loreto, held annually in December, is a highlight of the town's calendar, involving colorful processions, traditional dances, and elaborate religious ceremonies that attract pilgrims and visitors from far and wide. Other famous holidays include Semana Santa (Holy Week) and Dia de los Muertos (Day of the Dead), during which locals remember their ancestors with altars covered with marigolds, candles, and offerings of food and drink.

3. **Artisanal Crafts and Culinary Traditions:** Loreto's cultural fabric is woven with the threads of artisanal crafts and culinary traditions passed down through centuries. Visitors can visit bustling marketplaces and boutique stores stocked with handmade items, including

finely woven fabrics, handpainted pottery, and traditional Huichol beaded jewelry. Meanwhile, food connoisseurs may appreciate the flavors of Baja cuisine, with its emphasis on fresh seafood, locally produced ingredients, and timehonored traditions that represent the region's many cultural influences.

4. **Indigenous Heritage and Traditions:** Loreto's cultural diversity is complemented by the presence of indigenous communities, whose ancient traditions and languages continue to thrive in the modernday. Visitors can learn about the indigenous cultures of the region through immersive experiences, such as guided tours to nearby villages, where they can participate in traditional ceremonies, learn about traditional crafts, and engage with local artisans and storytellers who preserve the oral history and folklore of their ancestors.

5. **Environmental Conservation and Sustainability:** In recent years, Loreto has emerged as a leader in ecotourism and sustainable development, with a strong commitment to protecting its natural landscapes and marine ecosystems for future generations. Visitors can participate in ecofriendly activities, such as whale watching, sea turtle conservation programmes, and guided ecotours that promote responsible care of the environment.

6. **Cultural Exchange and Community Engagement:** Above all, Loreto's culture is marked by its warm hospitality and feeling of community, embracing guests with open arms and urging them to become part of the fabric of daily life in the town. Whether sharing stories over a cup of coffee with locals in a bustling cafe, joining in a traditional dance at a fiesta, or volunteering with local organizations to support community initiatives, visitors to Loreto are sure to leave with cherished memories and lasting connections that celebrate the rich weave of culture and heritage that defines this enchanting destination.

# Chapter 1: Planning Your Trip

## Best Time to Visit Loreto

Choosing the optimum time to visit Loreto depends on your preferences for weather, activity, and crowd levels. Loreto experiences a desert climate with pleasant temperatures year-round, yet there are distinct seasons that may influence your trip choices. Here's a summary of the ideal dates to visit Loreto based on numerous factors:

**1. Weather:**
*Peak Season (November to April):* This season is considered the finest time to visit Loreto, as the weather is delightfully warm and dry, with temperatures ranging from the mid-70s to mid-80s Fahrenheit (about 24-30°C). The skies are often clear, making it excellent for outdoor activities such as snorkeling, kayaking, hiking, and sightseeing. It's also the peak tourist season, so expect higher accommodation costs and more crowds, especially around holidays and festivals.
*Shoulder Seasons (May to October):* The shoulder seasons offer a mix of perks and cons. While temperatures can climb into the 90s Fahrenheit (30s

Celsius) or more during the summer months, the crowds thin out, and accommodation costs are frequently lower. If you can withstand the heat, you can still enjoy water activities and outdoor adventures, but be prepared for intermittent rain showers, especially in late summer and early fall.

## 2. **Wildlife Viewing:**

*Whale Watching (January to March):* Loreto is famed for its whale watching chances, particularly for sightings of gray whales that migrate to the warm waters of the Sea of Cortez to give birth. The ideal period for whale watching in Loreto is often from January to March, when these spectacular creatures can be viewed breaching and playing in the water.

*Sea Turtle Nesting (Late Summer to Early Fall):* If you're interested in observing sea turtle nesting and hatchling releases, plan your vacation to Loreto between late summer and early fall. Several conservation organizations in the area provide guided tours and educational programs to observe this natural phenomenon up close.

## 3. **Festivals and Events:**

*Feast of Our Lady of Loreto (December 8th):* This religious festival celebrates the patron saint of Loreto with colorful processions, traditional dances, and religious services hosted in the town's historic center. If you're interested in experiencing Loreto's cultural legacy and traditions, try visiting on this joyful occasion.

*Semana Santa (Holy Week):* Holy Week, leading up to Easter Sunday, is an important religious festival in Mexico, highlighted by processions, reenactments of the Passion of Christ, and special church services. Loreto has different events and activities throughout Semana Santa, making it a fascinating time to visit for cultural immersion.

4. **Diving and Snorkeling Conditions:**

*Calmer Seas (Spring and Fall):* If you're hoping to experience Loreto's underwater treasures through diving or snorkeling, consider travelling around the spring or fall when the sea conditions are often calmer. This provides for better visibility and more comfortable diving experiences, particularly for beginners.

The best time to visit Loreto depends on your interests for weather, activity, and cultural experiences. Whether you're seeking a sun-drenched beach break, wildlife encounters, or cultural immersion, Loreto provides something special year-round, so plan your trip accordingly to make the most of your time in this fascinating area.

# Visa Requirements and Travel Documents

Before going on your vacation to Loreto, it's crucial to verify you have the required visa requirements and travel paperwork in order to prevent any issues throughout your trip. Here's a guide to assist you negotiate the visa procedures and other travel paperwork for visiting Loreto:

1. **Passport:** All travellers to Loreto, Mexico, must possess a valid passport with at least six months' validity beyond their anticipated departure date. Ensure your passport is in good condition and has sufficient blank pages for entrance stamps.

2. **Visa Requirements:** Most visitors to Loreto, including citizens of the United States, Canada, the European Union, Australia, and many other countries, do not require a visa for tourist stays of up to 180 days. However, visa requirements differ based on your country and the purpose of your stay. It's crucial to verify the latest visa requirements for Mexico based on your citizenship before flying to Loreto.

3. **Tourist Card (FMM):** Upon arrival in Mexico, tourists traveling for tourism purposes will need to get a

Tourist Card, commonly known as an FMM (Forma Migratoria Multiple). The FMM permits for a stay of up to 180 days and must be filled out and shown to immigration authorities upon arrival. In some situations, the FMM fee may be included in the cost of your airline ticket, so be sure to check with your airline before leaving.

4. **Travel Insurance:** While not essential, it's highly recommended to obtain travel insurance that provides coverage for medical emergencies, trip cancellations, and other unforeseen occurrences. Medical care in Loreto can be expensive for travellers without insurance, so having enough coverage might provide peace of mind throughout your stay.

5. **Additional documents:** Depending on your travel conditions, you may need to produce additional documents upon admission to Mexico. This could include documentation of onward travel (such as a return flight ticket), proof of accommodation arrangements, and adequate finances to cover your stay. While these documents may not always be asked for, it's wise to have them readily available in case they're needed by immigration authorities.

6. **Check with the Mexican Embassy or Consulate**: For the most up-to-date and accurate information

regarding visa requirements and travel papers for visiting Loreto, it's suggested to contact the Mexican Embassy or Consulate in your country or visit their official website. They can provide particular assistance based on your nationality and individual travel conditions, helping you secure a smooth and hassle-free voyage to this wonderful place.

# Packing Tips for Your Loreto Adventure

Preparing for your vacation in Loreto takes careful consideration of what to pack to ensure you have all you need for a comfortable and pleasurable trip. Here are some crucial packing recommendations to help you prepare for your Loreto adventure:

1. **Lightweight and Breathable Clothing:** Pack lightweight and breathable clothing ideal for warm weather, including shorts, t-shirts, tank tops, sundresses, and swimwear. Choose moisture-wicking materials that dry fast and give UV protection to keep you cool and comfortable in the desert temperature.

2. **Sun Protection Essentials:** Don't forget to take sun protection items to safeguard yourself from the powerful

sun rays in Loreto. Include goods like sunscreen (SPF 30 or higher), sunglasses with UV protection, wide-brimmed hats or caps, and lightweight long-sleeve shirts for added sun protection.

3. **Water Gear:** If you want to indulge in water sports such as snorkeling, diving, or kayaking, make sure to carry water gear such as snorkel masks, fins, dive suits (if needed), and waterproof bags to keep your possessions dry. Consider bringing your own snorkel gear if you have it for enhanced comfort and hygiene.

4. **Comfortable Footwear:** Pack comfortable footwear ideal for walking, hiking, and exploring. Opt for robust sandals, swimming shoes, or lightweight hiking shoes that provide support and traction on different terrain. You may also want to carry a pair of flip-flops or beach sandals for relaxing by the pool or beach.

5. **Outdoor Essentials:** Don't forget to take outdoor basics for your travels in Loreto, like a lightweight daypack or backpack, reusable water bottle, bug repellant, and a small first-aid kit with basic supplies. If you plan to trek or visit distant locations, consider carrying a map, compass, or GPS gadget for navigation.

6. **Travel Documents and Essentials:** Ensure you have all necessary travel documents and essentials, including

your passport, tourist card (FMM), trip insurance information, airline tickets or e-tickets, and lodging reservations. Keep these documents organized and easily accessible during your travels.

7. **Electronics and Chargers:** Bring along vital equipment such as a smartphone, camera, or GoPro to capture memories of your Loreto experience. Don't forget to carry chargers, adapters, and power banks to keep your electronics powered throughout your vacation. Consider packing a waterproof cover or bag for your gadgets to safeguard them from water damage during aquatic sports.

8. **Spanish Phrasebook or Translator App**: While English is generally spoken in tourist areas in Loreto, having a basic command of Spanish might enhance your trip experience and help you communicate with locals. Consider packing a Spanish phrasebook or downloading a translating app on your smartphone for easy reference.

9. **Eco-Friendly Products:** Consider carrying eco-friendly products such as reusable water bottles, shopping bags, and toiletries containers to minimize your environmental effect during your trip. Avoid single-use plastics and opt for sustainable alternatives whenever possible.

10. **Cash and Credit Cards:** While credit cards are generally accepted in tourist areas of Loreto, it's advised to carry some cash in Mexican pesos for smaller purchases, tips, and emergencies. Bring a secure money belt or travel wallet to keep your cash and cards safe while sightseeing.

Don't forget to check the weather prediction and specific activity requirements before packing to personalise your packing list to your individual needs and preferences.

# Chapter 2: Getting to Loreto

## Transportation Options (Air, Road, Sea)

Loreto, located on the eastern coast of the Baja California Peninsula, is accessible by numerous forms of transportation, including air, road, and sea. Whether you're going domestically within Mexico or visiting from a foreign destination, there are various easy choices for accessing this charming town. Here's a guide to the transportation alternatives available for getting to Loreto:

1. **Air Travel:** *Loreto International Airport (LTO):* The principal gateway to Loreto is the Loreto International Airport (LTO), located roughly 15 minutes south of downtown Loreto. The airport serves internal flights from key cities in Mexico, including Mexico City, Tijuana, and Guadalajara, as well as international flights from certain destinations in the United States, such as Los Angeles and Phoenix. Airlines serving Loreto include Aeroméxico, Volaris, Alaska Airlines, and others. Upon arrival at the airport, you can rent a car, take a cab, or arrange for shuttle service to your accommodation in Loreto.

2. **Road Travel:** *Highway 1 (Carretera Transpeninsular):* If you want to go by vehicle, Highway 1, commonly known as the Carretera Transpeninsular, allows access to Loreto from various sections of Baja California Sur and mainland Mexico. The route covers the length of the Baja California Peninsula, linking Loreto to places such as La Paz, Cabo San Lucas, and Ensenada. Road conditions can vary, so be prepared for long expanses of desert landscape and little services along the way. If you're driving from the United States, you can cross the border at San Diego into Tijuana and then continue Highway 1 south to Loreto.

3. **Sea Travel:** *Ferry Service:* While there are no direct ferry lines to Loreto, you can go by ferry from the mainland port of Pichilingue, located near La Paz, to adjacent ports such as Santa Rosalía or Pichilingue. From there, you can drive to Loreto via Highway 1. Baja Ferries conducts ferry services between Pichilingue and Santa Rosalía, offering both passenger and car transit alternatives. Ferry timings and availability may vary, so it's advisable to check the latest information and book reservations in advance if traveling by water.

4. **Local Transportation:** *Taxis and Rental Cars*: Once you've arrived in Loreto, you can rely on taxis or rental automobiles to tour the town and neighbouring surroundings. Taxis are easily accessible at the airport

and throughout downtown Loreto, allowing easy transportation for short distances. If you prefer the option of having your own vehicle, various car rental businesses operate in Loreto, offering a selection of automobiles to fit your needs. Keep in mind that driving in Loreto is reasonably uncomplicated, with well-maintained roads and signage in Spanish.

No matter which transportation option you pick, arriving in Loreto is part of the trip, affording breathtaking views of the desert environment and coastal scenery along the route. Whether you come by air, road, or sea, you'll be greeted with great hospitality and numerous opportunities for discovery in this wonderful area.

## Airport Information and Ground Transportation

Arriving at Loreto International Airport (LTO) signals the beginning of your experience in this wonderful coastal town. Here's everything you need to know about Loreto's airport and ground transportation choices to help you negotiate your arrival and departure seamlessly:

1. **Loreto International Airport (LTO):**
   - *Location:* Loreto International Airport is situated roughly 15 minutes south of downtown Loreto, making it easily accessible for travelers arriving by air.
   - *Facilities:* The airport includes modern facilities, including a passenger terminal with check-in counters, baggage claim area, rental car offices, and amenities such as restaurants, stores, and restrooms.
   - *Airlines and Destinations:* Loreto International Airport services domestic and international flights run by airlines such as Aeroméxico, Volaris, Alaska Airlines, and others. Domestic destinations include Mexico City, Tijuana, Guadalajara, while international destinations include Los Angeles and Phoenix.
   - *Services:* The airport offers services such as currency exchange, ATMs, and vehicle rental organisations to satisfy the needs of passengers.

2. **Ground Transportation Options:**
   - *Taxis:* Taxis are widely accessible at Loreto International Airport, providing quick transportation to downtown Loreto and neighbouring areas. Taxi fares are either fixed or metered, and it's recommended to clarify the fare with the driver before starting your journey. Taxis

are a convenient choice for those with luggage or those seeking direct transportation to their accommodation.
- *Shuttle Services*: Some hotels and resorts in Loreto offer shuttle services to and from the airport for its visitors. If you've made prior arrangements with your accommodation, inquire about shuttle services and scheduling details to manage your airport transfer.
- *Rental Cars:* Rental car firms operate operations at Loreto International Airport, offering a selection of automobiles to suit your transportation needs. Renting a car allows flexibility and freedom to explore Loreto and its nearby attractions at your own speed. Be sure to book your rental car in advance and educate yourself with local traffic rules and regulations.
- *Public Transportation:* While there is limited public transportation available in Loreto, you may locate local buses or vans (known as colectivos) that travel between the airport and downtown Loreto. However, schedules and routes may be limited, so it's advisable to check in advance and be prepared for unexpected delays.

3. **Arrival and Departure Procedures:** Upon arrival at Loreto International Airport, follow signage to the

baggage claim area to get your luggage. Once you've collected your luggage, head to the passenger terminal exit, where you'll find ground transportation options such as taxis, shuttle services, and rental car counters.

When departing from Loreto, arrive at the airport well in advance of your scheduled departure time to allow for check-in, security screening, and boarding procedures. Be sure to check with your airline for specific check-in and baggage procedures.

## Border Crossing Information

If you're going to travel to Loreto from the United States, you'll likely cross the border into Mexico at one of the official border crossings along the US-Mexico border. Here's some vital border crossing information to help you prepare for your visit to Loreto:

1. **Border Crossing Points:** The most common border crossings from the United States into Mexico for passengers coming to Loreto are found in California's border cities, such as San Diego/Tijuana and Calexico/Mexicali. These crossings allow convenient access to route 1 (Carretera Transpeninsular), the principal route that crosses the length of the Baja California Peninsula, linking Loreto to other

communities in Baja California Sur and mainland Mexico.

2. **Required paperwork:** When crossing the border into Mexico by car, you'll need to submit specific paperwork at the immigration checkpoint. These often include:
- Valid passport: Ensure your passport has at least six months' validity beyond your anticipated departure date from Mexico.
- Tourist card (FMM): You may need to obtain a Tourist Card (Forma Migratoria Multiple, or FMM) upon entry into Mexico, depending on the length of your stay. The FMM permits for a stay of up to 180 days and must be filled out and given to immigration authorities.
- Vehicle registration and insurance: If you're driving your own vehicle into Mexico, you'll need to produce proof of vehicle registration and insurance coverage. Mexican auto insurance is needed for all automobiles going in Mexico, so be sure to get coverage before crossing the border.

3. **Crossing Procedures:** When reaching the border crossing, follow signage guiding you to the appropriate lanes for car traffic entering Mexico. Be prepared to halt at the immigration checkpoint, when you'll be required

to submit your documents to Mexican immigration officers.

Immigration agents may ask you questions about the purpose of your visit, your length of stay, and other pertinent details. Answer truthfully and submit any needed papers to speed the crossing process.

Once you've crossed immigration, go to the vehicle inspection section, where Mexican customs authorities may conduct a brief inspection of your vehicle. Be prepared to declare any items of value or commodities subject to customs duties, and follow any directions given by customs officers.

After completing the border crossing formalities, you'll be free to continue your drive on Highway 1 towards Loreto. Be sure to travel cautiously, obey traffic regulations, and follow directions signs to reach your location.

4. **Border Crossing Hours and Wait Times:** Border crossing hours and wait periods might vary depending on the time of day, day of the week, and season. It's advisable to check the latest border crossing information and wait times before your journey to plan your travel accordingly and avoid peak traffic periods.

5. **Travel Advisories and Safety Tips**: Before crossing the border into Mexico, acquaint yourself with any travel advisories or safety recommendations issued by the US

Department of State or other relevant authorities. Exercise caution and keep educated about local conditions and potential threats, especially in border areas.

# Chapter 3: Accommodation

## Luxury Resorts and Hotels

Loreto provides a collection of luxury resorts and hotels that cater to guests seeking elegant lodgings, superb service, and world-class amenities. Here are some top luxury resorts and hotels in Loreto to consider for your next indulgent getaway:

1. **Villa del Palmar Beach Resort & Spa at the Islands of Loreto:** Located on the pristine sands of Danzante Bay, Villa del Palmar Beach Resort & Spa offers exquisite accommodations surrounded by spectacular natural beauty. Guests can pick from spacious accommodations with ocean views, indulge in exquisite cuisine at on-site restaurants, and unwind with luxurious treatments at the award-winning Sabila Spa. The resort also boasts an abundance of outdoor activities, like golfing, kayaking, and snorkeling, making it an excellent destination for both relaxation and adventure.

2. **Loreto Bay Golf Resort & Spa at Baja:** Situated within the Loreto Bay National Marine Park, Loreto Bay Golf Resort & Spa offers an unequalled blend of luxury and quiet. The resort includes beautiful rooms and villas overlooking the Sea of Cortez, a championship golf

course designed by David Duval, and a full-service spa offering holistic treatments inspired by indigenous traditions. Guests can also enjoy excellent dining options, a glittering infinity pool, and access to neighbouring outdoor activities such as fishing, whale watching, and hiking.

3. **Danzante Bay Golf Resort & Spa:** Located between the Sierra de la Giganta mountains and the Sea of Cortez, Danzante Bay Golf Resort & Spa delivers an unparalleled luxury retreat in Loreto. The resort provides sumptuous suites with contemporary Mexican decor, world-class dining experiences showcasing local cuisines, and a range of recreational activities, including an infinity pool, tennis courts, and a fitness center. Guests can also tee off at the spectacular Rees Jones-designed golf course overlooking the coast, giving a tough yet scenic golfing experience.

4. **CostaBaja Resort & Spa:** Located just a short drive from downtown Loreto, CostaBaja Resort & Spa offers a quiet paradise of luxury and leisure. The resort has beautiful guest rooms and suites with spectacular views of the harbour or Sea of Cortez, upmarket dining options highlighting regional cuisine, and a full-service spa offering rejuvenating treatments inspired by Baja's natural surroundings. Guests can also have access to a private beach club, a marina with world-class fishing and

water sports activities, and a Gary Player-designed golf course overlooking the ocean.

5. **La Mision Loreto Hotel**: Situated on the waterfront promenade in downtown Loreto, La Mision Loreto Hotel offers a boutique luxury experience with individual attention and unique Mexican charm. The hotel has elegantly designed rooms and suites with balconies facing the sea or mountains, a rooftop pool and terrace with panoramic views, and a gourmet restaurant serving fresh seafood and regional specialties. Guests can also explore neighbouring attractions like historic missions, artisan stores, and stunning beaches within walking distance of the hotel.

These luxury resorts and hotels in Loreto offer the perfect blend of expensive lodgings, magnificent landscape, and great hospitality, providing a memorable and indulgent experience for discriminating tourists seeking the ultimate in luxury and leisure.

## BudgetFriendly Accommodations

If you're looking for budget-friendly hotels in Loreto without compromising comfort and convenience, there are various options available that give value for money and a comfortable stay. Here are some budget-friendly lodgings in Loreto to consider for your next trip:

1. **Posada de las Flores Loreto**: Posada de las Flores Loreto offers inexpensive elegance in the heart of downtown Loreto. This quaint boutique hotel has well-appointed rooms with traditional Mexican design, modern conveniences, and courtyard or garden views. Guests can enjoy complimentary continental breakfast, free Wi-Fi, and access to a rooftop patio with magnificent views of the old town and surrounding mountains. The hotel's central position enables easy access to nearby attractions, shops, and restaurants.

2. **Hotel Santa Fe Loreto:** Hotel Santa Fe Loreto is a budget-friendly alternative located only steps from the beachfront promenade in downtown Loreto. The motel offers pleasant guest rooms with modest decor, air conditioning, and flat-screen TVs. Guests can relax in the outdoor courtyard with a swimming pool and sun loungers or have a meal at the on-site restaurant providing authentic Mexican cuisine. The hotel also features complimentary Wi-Fi, parking, and 24-hour front desk assistance for added convenience.

3. **Loreto Playa Boutique Hotel:** Loreto Playa Boutique Hotel is a pleasant and economical hotel situated within walking distance of Loreto's main attractions and the Sea

of Cortez. The hotel has nicely appointed rooms with modern conveniences, including air conditioning, cable TV, and private bathrooms. Guests can repose in the hotel's courtyard garden or rest on the rooftop terrace with magnificent views of the town and surrounding mountains. Complimentary Wi-Fi and continental breakfast are included with your stay.

4. **Hotel Angra:** Hotel Angra offers budget-friendly lodgings in a handy position near Loreto's main square and historic sights. The motel has simple yet pleasant rooms with minimal facilities, like air conditioning, satellite TV, and private bathrooms. Guests can enjoy complimentary Wi-Fi, free parking, and a 24-hour front desk service. The hotel's central position gives easy access to restaurants, shops, and attractions within walking distance.

5. **Hotel Oasis Loreto:** Hotel Oasis Loreto provides cheap lodgings in a serene setting within a short drive from downtown Loreto. The hotel offers spacious rooms with comfy beds, air conditioning, and private balconies or patios facing the garden or pool area. Guests may relax by the outdoor swimming pool, have a meal at the on-site restaurant, or take advantage of services such as free Wi-Fi and daily continental breakfast.

These are ideal options for travelers seeking comfortable and economical lodging while seeing the natural beauty and cultural legacy of this quaint Mexican town. With their convenient locations, pleasant service, and value-added amenities, you may enjoy a wonderful stay in Loreto without breaking the budget.

## EcoFriendly Lodging Options

If you are an eco-conscious guest seeking environmentally sustainable housing options in Loreto, there are various eco-friendly establishments that prioritize conservation, renewable energy, and responsible tourism practices. Here are some eco-friendly accommodation options in Loreto that offer a green and sustainable stay:

1. **Loreto Bay National Park:** For a fully immersed eco-friendly experience, consider camping or glamping in Loreto Bay National Park. The park boasts clean beaches, crystal-clear waterways, and beautiful natural landscape, giving the perfect backdrop for eco-friendly camping and outdoor experiences. Several eco-conscious tour operators and lodgings provide guided camping trips and sustainable eco-tours in the park, allowing you

to connect with nature while limiting your environmental impact.

2. **Villa del Palmar at the Islands of Loreto:** Villa del Palmar in the Islands of Loreto is committed to sustainable practices and environmental conservation. The resort incorporates eco-friendly initiatives such as energy-efficient lighting, water conservation measures, waste reduction and recycling programs, and locally sourced organic products in its restaurants. Guests can also participate in eco-friendly activities such as snorkeling and kayaking tours, beach cleanups, and educational sessions on marine conservation and biodiversity.

3. **Loreto Playa Boutique Hotel:** Loreto Playa Boutique Hotel is a modest eco-friendly hotel located within walking distance of Loreto's main attractions and the Sea of Cortez. The hotel is committed to sustainability and environmental responsibility, with efforts such as energy-efficient lighting, water-saving fixtures, and eco-friendly cleaning solutions. Guests can enjoy comfortable lodgings with modern facilities, like free Wi-Fi and complimentary breakfast, while supporting environmentally sustainable practices.

4. **Posada de las Flores Loreto:** Posada de las Flores Loreto is a beautiful boutique hotel in downtown Loreto

that stresses sustainability and conservation. The hotel provides eco-friendly amenities such as energy-efficient lighting, solar-powered water heating, and organic toiletries. Guests can relax in the hotel's courtyard garden or rooftop terrace, which offers panoramic views of the old town and surrounding mountains. The hotel also supports local conservation efforts and community activities to increase environmental awareness.

5. **CostaBaja Resort & Spa:** CostaBaja Resort & Spa is a premium eco-friendly resort located just outside of Loreto, overlooking the Sea of Cortez. The resort is committed to sustainability and ethical tourist practices, including initiatives such as solar power generation, water conservation measures, and waste reduction programs. Guests can enjoy eco-friendly activities such as whale watching tours, snorkeling excursions, and nature treks, as well as sumptuous spa treatments using organic and locally produced products.

# Chapter 4: Exploring Loreto

## Top Attractions and Landmarks

Loreto, Mexico, offers a rich variety of natural beauty, cultural legacy, and outdoor adventures for visitors to explore and enjoy. Here are some of the top attractions and sites in Loreto that you won't want to miss during your visit:

1. **Loreto Bay National Marine Park**: One of Loreto's crown jewels, Loreto Bay National Marine Park is a UNESCO World Heritage Site famed for its pure seas, rich marine life, and magnificent surroundings. Visitors may snorkel, kayak, or paddleboard among vivid coral reefs, encounter sea lions and dolphins on boat trips, and explore hidden beaches accessible only by boat.

2. **Mission Nuestra Señora de Loreto:** Founded in 1697, Mission Nuestra Señora de Loreto is one of the earliest Spanish missions in Baja California Sur and a major historical landmark. The mission's baroque-style building, elegant façade, and peaceful courtyard offer an insight into Loreto's colonial past and religious tradition. Visitors can tour the mission's museum, which showcases relics, religious artwork, and historical exhibits.

3. **Malecón de Loreto (Loreto Waterfront Promenade):** Strolling along the Malecón de Loreto, or waterfront promenade, is a must-do activity for visitors to Loreto. Lined with palm trees, boutiques, restaurants, and art galleries, the Malecón offers breathtaking views of the Sea of Cortez and the famous silhouette of Isla Coronado. Visitors can enjoy leisurely hikes, beachfront dining, and vibrant sunsets against the backdrop of Loreto Bay.

4. **Islands of Loreto:** The Islands of Loreto, including Isla Coronado, Isla Carmen, and Isla Danzante, are a natural playground for outdoor enthusiasts and nature lovers. These uninhabited islands have pristine beaches, quiet coves, and rich wildlife, making them excellent for snorkeling, diving, kayaking, and wildlife viewing. Visitors can visit the islands on guided boat tours or day trips from Loreto.

5. **Danzante Bay Golf Club:** Set between the Sierra de la Giganta mountains and the Sea of Cortez, Danzante Bay Golf Club offers a demanding yet scenic golfing experience amidst spectacular natural splendour. Designed by renowned architect Rees Jones, the championship golf course boasts dramatic elevation changes, magnificent ocean views, and lush fairways framed by desert landscapes.

6. **Loreto Arches:** The Loreto Arches, popularly known as "Los Arcos," are renowned rock formations towering from the blue waters of Loreto Bay. These natural arches and sea stacks make a stunning setting for photography, sunset gazing, and exploring the surrounding marine life. Visitors can kayak or paddleboard around the arches, snorkel among colorful fish and corals, or simply observe the grandeur of this natural wonder from the shore.

7. **Sierra de la Giganta Mountains:** The Sierra de la Giganta mountains give a spectacular background to Loreto's landscape and offer chances for outdoor pursuits such as hiking, mountain biking, and birdwatching. Visitors may explore gorgeous trails, steep canyons, and secret waterfalls while immersing themselves in the region's rich biodiversity and geological wonders.

From pristine beaches and active marine life to ancient missions and gorgeous landscapes, Loreto provides a broad assortment of sights and sites ready to be discovered and explored.

# Hidden Gems Off the Beaten Path

Exploring Loreto's hidden gems off the usual road uncovers a world of natural beauty, cultural treasures, and secret oases waiting to be discovered by brave tourists. Here are some hidden gems in Loreto that offer unique experiences and opportunity for adventure:

1. **Puerto Escondido:** Tucked away on the eastern shore of Loreto Bay, Puerto Escondido is a hidden gem noted for its secluded coves, gorgeous beaches, and tranquil marina. Visitors may escape the crowds and enjoy kayaking, paddleboarding, or snorkeling in the crystal-clear waters of Puerto Escondido's sheltered harbour. The marina is also a portal to offshore fishing trips, wildlife encounters, and scenic boat tours of adjacent islands.

2. **San Javier Mission:** Located a picturesque drive inland from Loreto, the San Javier Mission is a hidden gem nestled in the foothills of the Sierra de la Giganta mountains. This magnificently restored mission, founded in 1699, has elegant baroque architecture, original artwork, and a calm courtyard garden. Visitors can explore the mission's mediaeval church, marvel at its beautiful embellishments, and soak in the tranquil aura of this hidden haven.

3. **Agua Verde:** For an off-the-grid adventure, venture south of Loreto to Agua Verde, a secluded fishing community set along the craggy coastline of the Sea of Cortez. Accessible by gravel road, Agua Verde provides clean beaches, blue waters, and breathtaking desert landscapes. Visitors can climb, swim, or simply rest on the beach, immersing themselves in the natural splendour of this hidden jewel.

4. **Mission San Bruno**: Hidden deep amid the desert environment north of Loreto, Mission San Bruno is a hidden treasure waiting to be discovered by brave travelers. Founded in 1699, this secluded mission is surrounded by harsh mountains and desert nature, affording a look into Baja California's colonial past and spiritual tradition. Visitors can trek or drive to the mission site and view its mediaeval church, cemetery, and ancient olive groves.

5. **Coronado Island (Isla Coronado):** While Isla Coronado is not wholly unknown, its gorgeous beaches, blue waters, and stunning rock formations make it a hidden jewel worth visiting. Located just offshore from Loreto, Coronado Island is accessible by boat or kayak and offers chances for snorkeling, diving, and wildlife watching. Visitors can climb to the island's picturesque

vistas, rest on secluded beaches, and encounter sea lions, dolphins, and migratory birds.

6. **Playa El Requesón:** Situated along the eastern coast of Loreto Bay, Playa El Requesón is a hidden gem noted for its peaceful sands, shallow waters, and panoramic views of the Sea of Cortez. This isolated beach is accessible by a short drive or boat ride from Loreto and offers chances for swimming, snorkeling, and beachcombing. Visitors can camp overnight on the beach and experience stunning sunrises and sunsets against the backdrop of Loreto's coastline.

## Guided Tours and Excursions

Embarking on guided tours and excursions in Loreto is a wonderful opportunity to discover the region's natural beauty, cultural legacy, and outdoor adventures with the expertise of local guides. Here are several guided tours and excursions in Loreto that offer remarkable experiences for travelers:

1. **Island Hopping and Snorkeling Tours:** Explore the pristine islands and marine sanctuaries of Loreto Bay National Marine Park on a guided island hopping and snorkeling tour. Local tour operators provide boat

excursions to surrounding islands such as Isla Coronado, Isla Carmen, and Isla Danzante, where you can snorkel among brilliant coral reefs, experience marine life such as sea lions and exotic fish, and relax on isolated beaches accessible only by boat.

2. **Whale Watching Expeditions:** Experience the thrill of whale viewing in Loreto's pristine seas on a guided whale watching tour. From December to April, gray whales come to the warm waters of the Sea of Cortez to give birth and nurse their young, affording great opportunity for up-close experiences. Local tour providers offer boat trips conducted by skilled instructors who provide insights into the behavior and biology of these gorgeous creatures.

3. **Kayaking and Paddleboarding Adventures:** Discover Loreto's gorgeous coastline and hidden coves on a guided kayaking or paddleboarding experience. Guided trips let you explore Loreto Bay's tranquil waters, rocky shoreline, and mangrove forests while learning about the region's environment and fauna from professional guides. Whether you're a beginner or experienced paddler, there are trips available at all ability levels, including sunset paddles, eco-tours, and multi-day expeditions.

4. **ATV and Off-Road Tours:** Embark on an adrenaline-fueled adventure through Loreto's rocky landscape on a guided ATV or off-road trip. Explore distant desert landscapes, mountain routes, and secret oases while crossing sandy washes and rocky terrain with skilled guides. ATV trips offer a thrilling opportunity to discover Loreto's natural beauty and off-the-beaten-path attractions, including breathtaking views, historic sites, and wildlife habitats.

5. **Cultural and Historical Tours:** Immerse yourself in Loreto's rich history and cultural legacy on a guided cultural and historical tour of the region. Visit historic monuments such as Mission Nuestra Señora de Loreto and San Javier Mission, explore local artisan markets and shops, and learn about traditional crafts, cuisine, and customs from experienced guides. Cultural tours offer insights into Loreto's colonial past, indigenous traditions, and present way of life.

6. **Fishing Charters and Sportfishing Expeditions:** Experience world-class fishing in the waters near Loreto on a guided fishing charter or sportfishing adventure. Whether you're a seasoned angler or rookie fisherman, local fishing charters provide guided trips to great fishing spots where you can reel in a variety of game fish, including dorado, yellowtail, marlin, and tuna. Expert captains and crew provide equipment, bait, and

instruction to ensure a successful and memorable fishing experience.

7. **Birdwatching and Eco-Tours:** Discover Loreto's unique birdlife and natural ecosystems on a guided birding and eco-tour conducted by knowledgeable naturalists. Explore coastal wetlands, desert oases, and mountain forests in search of resident and migratory bird species, including pelicans, herons, frigatebirds, and raptors. Guided eco-tours offer opportunities to learn about local ecosystems, conservation activities, and sustainable tourism practices while watching species in their natural habitat.

From island hopping and snorkeling to whale watching and cultural tours, there's no shortage of fascinating things awaiting you in this wonderful area.

# Chapter 5: Outdoor Adventures

## Snorkeling and Diving Spots

Loreto is blessed with an abundance of snorkeling and diving spots that showcase the region's rich marine biodiversity, vibrant coral reefs, and crystal-clear waters. Here are some top snorkeling and diving spots in Loreto that offer unforgettable underwater experiences:

1. **Coronado Island (Isla Coronado):** Coronado Island is renowned for its spectacular underwater scenery, including colorful coral gardens, rocky reefs, and diverse marine life. Snorkelers and divers can explore shallow reefs teeming with tropical fish, sea turtles, and moray eels, as well as deeper waters inhabited by larger marine species such as rays, sharks, and dolphins. The island's clear waters and calm conditions make it an ideal spot for snorkeling and diving year-round.

2. **Danzante Bay:** Danzante Bay boasts some of the clearest and most pristine waters in Loreto, making it a popular destination for snorkeling and diving enthusiasts. The bay is home to a variety of underwater habitats, including rocky reefs, sandy bottoms, and seagrass beds, which support a diverse array of marine

life. Snorkelers and divers can encounter colorful reef fish, octopuses, sea stars, and other fascinating creatures while exploring Danzante Bay's underwater wonders.

3. **Loreto Bay National Marine Park:** Loreto Bay National Marine Park encompasses a vast expanse of protected waters teeming with marine biodiversity and natural beauty. The marine park offers numerous snorkeling and diving sites, including shallow reefs, underwater pinnacles, and submerged rock formations, where divers can encounter an array of marine life, including tropical fish, rays, sea lions, and whale sharks. Popular dive sites within the marine park include El Bajo, Punta Lobos, and Las Islas.

4. **Punta Nopolo:** Punta Nopolo is a picturesque coastal area located just south of Loreto, known for its pristine beaches and excellent snorkeling opportunities. The sheltered coves and rocky reefs of Punta Nopolo provide ideal conditions for snorkelers to explore vibrant coral gardens, rocky outcrops, and underwater caves inhabited by a variety of marine species, including colorful reef fish, sea turtles, and invertebrates.

5. **Isla del Carmen:** Isla del Carmen, the largest island in the Loreto Bay National Marine Park, offers exceptional snorkeling and diving opportunities along its rocky shores and secluded bays. The island's underwater

terrain features dramatic drop-offs, underwater caves, and vertical walls adorned with colorful corals and sponges, creating a stunning backdrop for underwater exploration. Snorkelers and divers can encounter schools of fish, pelagic species, and other marine creatures while exploring Isla del Carmen's underwater realms.

6. **Puerto Escondido**: Puerto Escondido, a tranquil bay located just south of Loreto, is a hidden gem for snorkeling and diving enthusiasts seeking off-the-beaten-path adventures. The bay's crystal-clear waters and rocky reefs provide habitat for a variety of marine life, including tropical fish, octopuses, and sea stars. Snorkelers can explore the bay's shallow waters and rocky shoreline, while divers can venture deeper to discover underwater caves, canyons, and swim-throughs.

From colorful coral reefs and rocky outcrops to encounters with sea lions and whale sharks, snorkeling and diving in Loreto promise unforgettable experiences for nature lovers and adventure seekers alike.

## Hiking Trails and Nature Reserves

Loreto is surrounded by spectacular natural settings, including mountains, desert, and coastal areas, giving a range of hiking paths and environmental reserves for outdoor enthusiasts to explore. Here are some top hiking trails and natural areas near Loreto:

1. **Sierra de la Giganta Mountains**: The Sierra de la Giganta mountains provide a spectacular background to Loreto's environment and offer several hiking options for nature enthusiasts. Explore picturesque paths that snake through steep gorges, towering peaks, and desert oases, affording panoramic views of the surrounding scenery and sightings of native animals such as bighorn sheep, roadrunners, and desert birds. Popular hiking locations in the Sierra de la Giganta include the San Javier Mission Trail, Tabor Canyon, and the Loreto Mountain Range.

2. **Parque Nacional Bahía de Loreto (Loreto Bay National Park):** Loreto Bay National Park is a protected marine and terrestrial area that comprises a varied range of habitats, including coastal dunes, mangrove forests, and desert landscapes. The park provides various hiking paths that run through pure wilderness areas, allowing opportunity to observe natural flora and fauna, such as cactus, birds, and reptiles. Hike along coastal cliffs,

sandy beaches, and rocky shorelines while enjoying beautiful views of the Sea of Cortez and adjacent islands.

3. **Parque Nacional Sierra de la Laguna (Sierra de la Laguna National Park):** Located south of Loreto, Sierra de la Laguna National Park is a UNESCO Biosphere Reserve famed for its lush woods, waterfalls, and biodiversity. The park includes a network of hiking paths that run through verdant canyons, pine-oak forests, and harsh mountain terrain, allowing opportunity to explore hidden waterfalls, natural pools, and panoramic vistas. Hikers can explore paths such as the Rancho La Trinidad Loop, Barranca de la Zorra, and La Laguna de la Media Luna.

4. **San Basilio Arroyo and Petroglyphs:** San Basilio Arroyo is a picturesque canyon located just outside of Loreto, famed for its ancient rock art and spectacular desert vistas. Hike along the arroyo's sandy wash and granite cliffs to see prehistoric petroglyphs, rock shelters, and archaeological sites left behind by indigenous tribes. Guided tours are provided to explore the area's cultural and natural history while learning about the significance of the petroglyphs and their relationship to the region's indigenous peoples.

5. **Parque Nacional Bahía Concepción (Conception Bay National Park):** Conception Bay National Park is a

natural coastal area located north of Loreto, famed for its quiet beaches, blue waters, and scenic hiking routes. Explore pathways that snake through coastal dunes, mangrove forests, and desert scrub, affording opportunities to view native wildlife such as shorebirds, marine animals, and reptiles. Hike to secret coves and views overlooking the bay, where you may rest, swim, or enjoy a picnic amidst the natural splendour of the park.

6. **La Giganta Eco-Aventuras:** La Giganta Eco-Aventuras offers guided hiking excursions and eco-tours that explore Loreto's unique ecosystems and cultural history. Join professional guides on walks to remote desert canyons, mountain summits, and coastal bluffs, while learning about the region's geology, vegetation, and fauna. Hiking tours are provided for all skill levels, from relaxing nature walks to demanding peak climbs, delivering remarkable experiences for outdoor enthusiasts of all ages.

Lace up your hiking boots, pack lots of water and sunscreen, and embark on a journey to see the natural treasures of this magnificent area in Baja California Sur, Mexico.

# Fishing Charters and Water Sports

Loreto is a paradise for fishing aficionados and water sports lovers, offering a wide selection of fishing excursions and water sports activities for guests to enjoy. Here are some popular options for fishing charters and water sports in Loreto:

1. **Fishing Charters:** Loreto is recognised for its world-class sportfishing prospects, with abundant marine life and different fishing grounds in the Sea of Cortez. Join a fishing trip led by expert captains and crew who know the finest areas for capturing trophy fish such as dorado, yellowtail, marlin, and tuna. Whether you're a novice angler or seasoned fisherman, fishing charters in Loreto provide half-day, full-day, and multi-day experiences suited to your tastes and skill level.

2. **Kayaking:** Explore Loreto's gorgeous coastline and peaceful bays by kayak on a guided kayaking adventure. Paddle around isolated beaches, rugged shorelines, and mangrove forests while soaking in stunning views of the Sea of Cortez and adjacent islands. Kayaking experiences are provided for all ability levels, from relaxing paddles in calm seas to ambitious adventures exploring secret coves and marine sanctuaries.

3. **Stand-up Paddleboarding (SUP):** Stand-up paddleboarding (SUP) is a popular water sport in Loreto, offering a pleasant and peaceful way to explore the region's pristine waters. Rent a paddleboard and float across the surface of Loreto Bay, enjoying panoramic views of the coastline and marine life below. Join a guided SUP tour to paddle to isolated beaches, snorkeling areas, and breathtaking overlooks while learning about the area's ecology and history from professional guides.

4. **Snorkeling and Scuba Diving**: Discover Loreto's underwater delights on a snorkeling or scuba diving excursion in the crystal-clear waters of the Sea of Cortez. Dive among brilliant coral reefs, rocky outcrops, and underwater pinnacles rich with colorful marine life, including tropical fish, sea turtles, and rays. Guided snorkeling and diving experiences are provided for all skill levels, with opportunities to explore shallow reefs near to shore or journey to farther offshore sites.

5. **Whale Watching Tours:** Experience the thrill of witnessing majestic whales in their natural habitat on a whale watching cruise in Loreto. From December to April, gray whales come to the warm waters of the Sea of Cortez to give birth and nurse their young, affording great opportunity for up-close experiences. Join a guided whale watching excursion led by skilled captains who

know the finest areas to witness these amazing creatures breaching, tail-slapping, and playing in the sea.

6. **Jet Skiing and Water Sports Rentals:** Rent a jet ski or other water sports equipment and enjoy adrenaline-pumping thrills on the seas of Loreto Bay. Zip across the surface of the sea, feeling the wind in your hair and the spray of seawater on your skin, as you explore hidden coves, offshore islands, and gorgeous coastal areas. Jet skiing and water sports rentals are offered at certain beach resorts and marinas in Loreto, offering fun-filled activities for families, couples, and thrill-seekers alike.

7. **Sailing and Yachting:** Set sail on a sailing or yachting experience in Loreto Bay, discovering the region's pristine waters and gorgeous shoreline aboard a private yacht or sailboat. Charter a luxury boat for a day of leisurely cruising, snorkeling, and sunbathing, or join a guided sailing excursion to explore hidden coves, marine sanctuaries, and secluded islands. Sailing and yachting charters in Loreto offer bespoke experiences tailored to your tastes, whether you're seeking relaxation, adventure, or romance on the sea.

# Chapter 6: Immersing Yourself in Culture

## Museums and Art Galleries

Immerse yourself in Loreto's rich cultural legacy and artistic traditions by visiting its museums and art galleries, which display the region's history, artistry, and local talent. Here are some major museums and art galleries to explore in Loreto:

1. **Museo de las Misiones (Museum of the Missions):** Located in the centre of Loreto, the Museo de las Misiones is housed in a historic edifice that originally served as a Jesuit mission and monastery. The museum shows relics, artwork, and historical documents linked to the missions established by Spanish missionaries in Baja California Sur during the colonial era. Visitors can learn about the region's indigenous cultures, colonial history, and religious legacy through interactive exhibits, archaeological displays, and multimedia presentations.

2. **Galería de Arte Tonantzin:** Galería de Arte Tonantzin is a modern art gallery located in downtown Loreto, displaying the work of local and regional artists.

The gallery displays a broad variety of paintings, sculptures, ceramics, and mixed-media artwork inspired by the natural beauty, cultural traditions, and everyday life of Baja California Sur. Visitors can tour rotating exhibitions, meet the artists, and purchase unique artworks as souvenirs or gifts.

3. **Casa de la Cultura de Loreto (House of Culture):** Casa de la Cultura de Loreto is a cultural institution dedicated to preserving and promoting the arts, crafts, and traditions of Loreto and its surrounding regions. The center hosts art exhibitions, workshops, and cultural events throughout the year, exhibiting the talents of local artists, singers, dancers, and performers. Visitors can participate in hands-on activities like painting, ceramics, and traditional crafts, or enjoy live performances and cultural events.

4. **Museo de Arte de Loreto (Loreto Art Museum):** The Museo de Arte de Loreto is a tiny art museum located along the seaside promenade in downtown Loreto. The museum includes a variety of contemporary and traditional artwork by local and regional artists, including paintings, sculptures, and textiles. Visitors can appreciate paintings that reflect the natural beauty, cultural heritage, and colourful spirit of Baja California Sur, as well as learn about the artists and their creative processes.

5. **Baja Bohemia Art Gallery:** Baja Bohemia Art Gallery is a delightful gallery and cultural venue located in downtown Loreto, presenting the work of local and international artists. The collection contains a broad range of paintings, photography, jewelry, and handicrafts inspired by the beauty and culture of Baja California Sur. Visitors can peruse unique artworks, meet the artists, and learn about the creative culture blooming in Loreto and its surrounding surroundings.

6. **Galería La Giganta:** Galería La Giganta is an art gallery and studio space dedicated to promoting the arts and culture of Loreto and the surrounding region. The gallery highlights the work of local artists and craftspeople, including paintings, pottery, textiles, and photography, as well as hosts exhibitions, workshops, and cultural events throughout the year. Visitors can browse the gallery's unique collection, meet the artists, and purchase handcrafted products and souvenirs manufactured by local artisans.

7. **Museo Comunitario de Loreto (Community Museum of Loreto)**: The Museo Comunitario de Loreto is a community museum dedicated to conserving and sharing the history, customs, and cultural legacy of Loreto and its citizens. The museum offers displays on local history, archaeology, and natural resources, as well

as artifacts, photographs, and oral histories reflecting the region's past and present. Visitors can learn about the different cultures, lifestyles, and contributions of the people who call Loreto home.

Explore Loreto's museums and art galleries to explore the rich display of history, culture, and creativity that defines this dynamic resort in Baja California Sur, Mexico. Whether you're interested in colonial history, contemporary art, or traditional crafts, there's something for everyone to enjoy and appreciate in Loreto's cultural scene.

## Traditional Festivals and Events

Experience the vibrant culture and rich traditions of Loreto by participating in its traditional festivals and activities, which commemorate the region's heritage, religious beliefs, and community spirit. Here are some notable festivals and events in Loreto that you won't want to miss:

1. **Festival de la Virgen de Loreto (Festival of the Virgin of Loreto):** Held annually on September 8th, the Festival de la Virgen de Loreto is a religious feast honoring the patron saint of Loreto, Our Lady of Loreto.

The celebration incorporates religious processions, Masses, and cultural acts, as well as traditional music, dance, and fireworks. Pilgrims from near and far assemble to pay respect to the Virgin Mary and seek her blessings for health, prosperity, and protection.

2. **Carnaval de Loreto (Loreto Carnival):** Carnaval de Loreto is a spectacular celebration observed in the weeks leading up to Lent, with colorful parades, music, dancing, and street performers. The carnival activities include traditional costumes, masks, and floats, as well as exciting music, food, and entertainment for all ages. Visitors can join in the festivities, participate in costume contests, and eat excellent local cuisine during this joyous celebration of community and culture.

3. **Semana Santa (Holy Week):** Semana Santa, or Holy Week, is a sacred holiday remembering the Passion, Death, and Resurrection of Jesus Christ, commemorated with religious processions, Masses, and rituals. In Loreto, Semana Santa is a time of spiritual reflection and devotion, with church services, processions, and reenactments of biblical events taking place throughout the week. Visitors can observe the solemnity and pageantry of Semana Santa while experiencing the kindness and warmth of the local community.

4. **Dia de los Muertos (Day of the Dead):** Dia de los Muertos is a Mexican celebration honoring deceased loved ones and celebrating the continuity of life and death. In Loreto, Dia de los Muertos is commemorated with altars, offerings, and commemoration ceremonies in homes, graves, and public areas. Visitors can engage in cultural activities such as altar decorating, sugar skull painting, and traditional music and dance performances, as well as experience traditional dishes and beverages related with the event.

5. **Fiestas Patrias (Independence Day):** Fiestas Patrias, or Mexican Independence Day, is celebrated with patriotic zeal and national pride on September 16th, marking Mexico's declaration of independence from Spanish domination in 1810. In Loreto, Fiestas Patrias is highlighted with colorful parades, music, dancing, and fireworks, as well as traditional cuisine, drinks, and cultural celebrations. Visitors can join in the ceremonies, see the hoisting of the Mexican flag, and experience the joyous ambiance of this important national event.

6. **Feria de Loreto (Loreto Fair):** The Feria de Loreto is an annual fair and cultural celebration highlighting the history, traditions, and customs of Loreto and its surrounding regions. The fair contains agricultural displays, livestock shows, artisan markets, and culinary competitions, as well as live music, dancing

performances, and amusement attractions. Visitors can sample local foods, shop handmade goods, and enjoy entertainment for the whole family during this lively celebration of Loreto's cultural legacy.

7. **Fiesta de San Javier (Feast of San Javier)**: The Fiesta de San Javier is a religious feast celebrating Saint Francis Xavier, the patron saint of the nearby mission town of San Javier. The celebration incorporates religious processions, Masses, and prayers, as well as traditional music, dance, and food. Visitors can discover the spiritual devotion and cultural traditions of the local community while enjoying the lively ambiance of this annual celebration.

From religious festivals and cultural celebrations to patriotic holidays and community fairs, Loreto provides a broad selection of traditional events and festivities that display the region's colourful culture and heritage. If you're seeking spiritual development, cultural immersion, or festive fun, there's something for everyone to enjoy and experience in Loreto's bustling schedule of traditional festivals and activities.

# Interaction with Local Communities

Interacting with local populations in Loreto offers guests a deeper insight of the region's culture, traditions, and way of life. Here are some ways to engage with local communities and immerse yourself in the authentic charm of Loreto:

1. **Attend Community Events and Festivals:** Participate in local festivals, fiestas, and cultural events where you may mix with residents, enjoy traditional music and dance performances, and try regional cuisine. Look for events like Dia de los Muertos celebrations, Carnaval de Loreto, and Fiestas Patrias to enjoy the vivid energy and warmth of the local community.

2. **Visit Artisan Markets and Workshops:** Explore artisan markets, craft fairs, and workshops where local artisans present their handmade wares, including ceramics, textiles, jewelry, and artwork. Strike up talks with artists, learn about their creative skills and cultural inspirations, and purchase original souvenirs to support local artisans and their families.

3. **Participate in Cultural Workshops and Classes:** Take part in cultural workshops and classes that offer hands-on experiences in traditional activities such as

cooking, pottery-making, dance, and music. Learn from local experts and practitioners who can teach you the skills and practices passed down through generations, providing insight into the cultural legacy and customs of Loreto.

4. **Volunteer with Community Organizations:** Volunteer your time and skills with community organizations, nonprofits, or conservation groups working to promote local initiatives, environmental conservation, or social welfare programmes. Engage in meaningful activities such as beach cleanups, community gardening, or educational initiatives that help the local community and environment.

5. **Participate in Homestay or Community-Based Tourism Programs:** Stay with local families or participate in community-based tourism programs that offer immersive cultural experiences and opportunity to connect with inhabitants on a personal level. Live like a local, share meals with your hosts, and participate in daily activities and traditions, gaining insight into the daily rhythms and customs of life in Loreto.

6. **Explore Off-the-Beaten-Path Neighborhoods and Villages:** Venture beyond tourist destinations and discover off-the-beaten-path neighborhoods, villages, and rural settlements where you may connect with

residents and experience everyday life in Loreto. Strike up conversations with locals at markets, parks, or common gathering spots, and be open to learning about their stories, perspectives, and experiences.

7. **Support Local Businesses and Entrepreneurs:** Patronize locally-owned businesses, restaurants, cafes, and shops that exhibit the talents, flavors, and goods of Loreto's neighbourhoods. Engage with shop owners, craftsmen, and entrepreneurs, and hear about the unique stories behind their enterprises and the importance of supporting local economies and livelihoods.

Interacting with local communities in Loreto gives guests real and enriching experiences that build cultural exchange, mutual respect, and deep connections.

# Chapter 7: Dining and Nightlife

## Restaurants Serving Authentic Cuisine

Savoring the original flavors of Loreto's cuisine is a delightful gastronomic adventure that delivers a taste of the region's culinary heritage and local ingredients. Here are several restaurants in Loreto noted for delivering traditional Baja California Sur cuisine:

1. **El Rey del Taco:** Indulge in authentic Mexican street food at El Rey del Taco, a popular taqueria known for its tasty tacos, burritos, and quesadillas. Choose from a variety of fillings, including grilled meats, seafood, and vegetarian options, and customize your order with fresh salsas and toppings. Don't miss the opportunity to enjoy local favourites such as fish tacos, shrimp ceviche, and carne asada.

2. **La Palapa Restaurant:** Enjoy fresh seafood and regional dishes with spectacular views of Loreto Bay at La Palapa Restaurant, located within a beachside resort. Feast on meals such as ceviche, fish tacos, shrimp cocktails, and grilled catch of the day, cooked using locally sourced ingredients and traditional traditions.

Pair your meal with a cool margarita or local craft beer for the ideal dining experience.

3. **Mi Loreto:** Experience the flavors of Baja California Sur cuisine at Mi Loreto, a tiny restaurant specialised in regional specialties crafted with locally sourced ingredients. Feast on traditional favorites like machaca with huevos (shredded beef with eggs), chiles rellenos (stuffed peppers), and enchiladas de mole (mole enchiladas), complemented by handmade tortillas and fresh salsa. Save room for homemade treats like flan or tres leches cake to conclude your meal.

4. **La Picazon:** La Picazon gives a taste of real Mexican cuisine in a casual and pleasant ambiance. Sample cuisine inspired by the flavors of Baja California Sur, such as grilled fish tacos, seafood drinks, and hearty beef entrees served with rice, beans, and tortillas. Be sure to taste their distinctive dishes like pescado zarandeado (grilled fish marinated in adobo sauce) and camarones al mojo de ajo (garlic shrimp).

5. **El Corazon Cafe:** El Corazon Cafe is a beautiful cafe and bakery noted for its superb breakfast and brunch dishes, including freshly baked pastries, omelets, and breakfast burritos. Sip on locally roasted coffee or freshly squeezed juices while enjoying the laid-back ambiance and courteous service. Don't miss their

distinctive meals like chilaquiles, huevos rancheros, and breakfast enchiladas cooked with real Mexican flavors.

6. **La Mision Restaurante:** La Mision Restaurante offers an elegant dining experience with a focus on traditional Mexican cuisine and international delicacies. Dine in a magnificent courtyard setting surrounded by lush gardens and colonial buildings while tasting meals like mole poblano, cochinita pibil, and grilled seafood platters. Pair your meal with a range of Mexican wines, specialty cocktails, or artisanal mezcal for an unforgettable dining experience.

7. **El Charco Azul:** El Charco Azul is a family-owned restaurant specializing in seafood dishes and Mexican classics, presented in a casual and pleasant ambiance. Feast on fresh ceviche, shrimp cocktails, fish tacos, and seafood soups created with locally sourced ingredients and robust tastes. Enjoy views of the marina and waterfront while dining on the outdoor terrace or indoor dining area.

Indulge in the original flavors of Baja California Sur cuisine at these restaurants in Loreto, where you can sample the region's culinary delicacies and enjoy a true sense of Mexico's gourmet legacy. These places offer a wonderful dining experience that highlights the rich flavors and cultural diversity of Loreto's culinary scene.

# Bars and Nightclubs for Evening Entertainment

Experience the busy nightlife of Loreto at these bars and nightclubs, where you can unwind with refreshing beverages, loud music, and nice company:

1. **1697 Loreto Bar:** Located in the centre of downtown Loreto, 1697 Loreto Bar is a popular destination for locals and tourists alike to enjoy cocktails, live music, and a lively atmosphere. Sip on innovative cocktails created with local ingredients while socialising with fellow visitors and dancing to the beats of live bands or DJs. The bar's outside terrace offers amazing views of Loreto Bay, making it the perfect location to relax and unwind after a day of exploring.

2. **La Perla Negra Cantina**: La Perla Negra Cantina is a famous local watering place known for its laid-back ambiance, courteous service, and broad assortment of drinks. Pull up a stool at the bar and enjoy ice-cold beers, artisan cocktails, and top-shelf spirits while mingling with locals and fellow tourists. The cantina typically holds live music performances, karaoke nights, and other events, providing entertainment for customers of all ages.

3. **Tio Lupe's Beach Club:** Tio Lupe's Beach Club is a beachfront bar and restaurant located just steps away from the shores of Loreto Bay. Relax in a hammock or lounge chair on the sandy beach while sipping on tropical cocktails and enjoying magnificent views of the Sea of Cortez. The beach club typically offers sunset parties, bonfires, and live music events, creating a laid-back ambiance great for unwinding and enjoying the beauty of Loreto's coastline.

4. **Bandido's Bar & Grill:** Bandido's Bar & Grill is a vibrant sports bar and restaurant where you can catch the game on big-screen TVs, play billiards, and enjoy a broad range of beers, cocktails, and pub fare. Cheer on your favorite team while relishing delectable appetizers, burgers, and tacos, or challenge your pals to a game of darts or foosball. Bandido's regularly conducts quiz evenings, theme parties, and live music performances for customers to enjoy.

5. **Oasis Bar:** Oasis Bar is a popular destination for nighttime entertainment, offering a calm environment, live music, and excellent drinks. Situated within a beachside resort, the bar includes outside seating overlooking the pool and gardens, providing a calm backdrop to drink cocktails, beers, and wines. Guests may unwind with nightly entertainment, including live

music, DJ sets, and special events, making it a favorite gathering area for travellers and residents alike.

6. **El Santuario Bar & Restaurant:** El Santuario Bar & Restaurant offers a classy setting for evening beverages and dining, with a focus on craft cocktails, exquisite wines, and gourmet cuisine. Located within a boutique hotel, the bar has an attractive indoor lounge and outdoor terrace with spectacular views of the surrounding mountains and gardens. Savor inventive cocktails crafted with quality spirits and fresh ingredients while enjoying live music or DJ sets in a sophisticated and stylish setting.

7. **Marina Loreto Bar & Grill:** Marina Loreto Bar & Grill is a waterfront restaurant and bar located in the Loreto Marina, with beautiful views of the harbor and Sea of Cortez. Relax on the outside patio or rooftop terrace while sipping on drinks, margaritas, or refreshing beers and watching the boats come and go. The pub typically organises live music performances, happy hour promotions, and themed events, providing a lively and joyful atmosphere for patrons to enjoy.

Experience the active nightlife of Loreto at these bars and nightclubs, where you can enjoy tasty cocktails, live music, and good times with friends old and new. Whether you're looking for a laid-back beach vibe or a frenetic dance floor, these places provide something for everyone to enjoy while soaking in the beauty and excitement of Loreto after dark.

## Street Food and Culinary Experiences

Explore the gastronomic wonders of Loreto's street food scene and culinary experiences, where you can sample authentic flavors, local delicacies, and delectable dishes cooked with fresh ingredients. Here are some must-try street food sellers and gastronomic experiences in Loreto:

1. **Tacos de Pescado (Fish Tacos) Stands**: Indulge in the signature flavors of Baja California Sur with tacos de pescado (fish tacos) from street food kiosks and vendors strewn throughout Loreto. Feast on crunchy battered fish, fresh salsa, cabbage slaw, and creamy sauces served on warm corn tortillas for a delicious and savoury lunch. Look for stalls near the waterfront or in downtown neighbourhoods for the freshest and most flavorful fish tacos in town.

2. **Mariscos (Seafood) Stands and Food Trucks**: Sample a selection of mariscos (seafood) specialties

from food trucks and stands serving ceviche, aguachile, shrimp cocktails, and seafood tostadas. Taste the freshness of locally caught fish, marinated in citrus juices and spices, and served with crisp tostadas or tortilla chips for a refreshing and tasty delight. Don't miss the opportunity to enjoy marlin tacos, clam drinks, and octopus ceviche for a flavour of the sea.

3. **Elotes (Mexican Street Corn) Stands:** Enjoy the savory and spicy flavors of elotes (Mexican street corn) from sellers selling grilled corn on the cob slathered with mayonnaise, cheese, chili powder, and lime juice. Sink your teeth into juicy kernels of corn brimming with flavor and topped with tangy and flavorful toppings for a tasty and fulfilling snack. Look for elotes stands at local markets, parks, and street corners for a wonderful and authentic street food experience.

4. **Fruit Stands and Agua Fresca Carts:** Stay refreshed and hydrated with fresh fruit from street sellers and carts offering an assortment of seasonal fruits, cut and served with chili powder, salt, and lime juice for a spicy and refreshing snack. Wash down your fruit with agua fresca, a classic Mexican beverage made with fresh fruit, water, and a touch of sweetness, available in flavors like watermelon, pineapple, and cucumber for a cool and refreshing treat.

5. **Churro Stands and Sweet Treats**: Indulge your sweet taste with churros, a renowned Mexican street food staple, from sellers selling freshly fried doughnuts coated in cinnamon sugar and served with chocolate sauce or caramel for dipping. Bite into crispy and golden churros filled with dulce de leche or Nutella for an extra delicious treat, great for satisfying your desires and indulging in a sweet gourmet experience.

6. **Cooking Classes and Market Tours:** Immerse yourself in Loreto's culinary culture with cooking courses and market trips that give hands-on experiences and insights into traditional Mexican food. Join local chefs and culinary experts to learn how to cook regional dishes utilising fresh ingredients from local markets and sellers, and obtain a greater appreciation of the flavors, methods, and traditions of Baja California Sur cuisine.

7. **Street Food Tours and Food Carts:** Embark on a street food tour or explore food carts and sellers on your own to find hidden treasures and local favorites serving up authentic flavors and gastronomic delights. Wander through crowded markets, colourful plazas, and lively streetscapes to enjoy a range of street meals, snacks, and treats while taking in the sights, sounds, and fragrances of Loreto's dynamic food scene.

Experience the flavors and culinary sensations of Loreto's street food scene, where you can savor original flavors, local delicacies, and delectable dishes cooked with fresh ingredients from the sea and land. Whether you're indulging in fish tacos, seafood ceviche, or sweet churros, these gastronomic delicacies offer a glimpse of Baja California Sur's rich culinary heritage and vibrant street food culture.

# Chapter 8: Shopping in Loreto

## Local Markets and Souvenir Shops

Discover the colourful local markets and souvenir stores in Loreto, where you can buy a range of items, artisan crafts, and unique souvenirs to commemorate your visit. Here are some must-visit marketplaces and shops in Loreto:

1. **Mercado Municipal de Loreto (Loreto Municipal Market):** Explore the bustling stalls and bright atmosphere of the Mercado Municipal de Loreto, where you can shop for fresh fruit, seafood, meats, spices, and local delicacies. Browse through colorful displays of fruits, veggies, and homemade goods, and connect with local sellers offering traditional crafts, apparel, jewelry, and souvenirs. Don't miss the chance to sample regional foods, spices, and snacks while touring this vibrant market.

2. **Artisan Market in Plaza Civica:** Visit the Artisan Market in Plaza Civica, located in the heart of downtown Loreto, where you can browse for handmade crafts, textiles, pottery, and artwork created by local artisans. Browse around stalls stocked with colorful textiles, woven baskets, pottery, and traditional Mexican

handicrafts, and find unique items to take home as keepsakes of your stay. Chat with craftsmen and learn about their craft processes and cultural heritage while supporting local craftsmanship.

3. **Tianguis Artesanal (Artisan Market) in Malecón:** Stroll down the Malecón promenade and visit the Tianguis Artesanal (Artisan Market), a seasonal market showcasing a range of handcrafted products, jewelry, apparel, and souvenirs manufactured by local craftsmen. Browse among stalls selling beaded jewelry, leather goods, embroidered linens, and decorative things, and find one-of-a-kind treasures to remind you of your stay in Loreto. Enjoy live music, street performances, and cultural events while shopping at this vibrant market by the sea.

4. **Marina Mercado Artesanal (Marina Artisan Market):** Explore the Marina Mercado Artesanal, a waterfront market located near the Loreto Marina, where you can buy artisan goods, gifts, and souvenirs while enjoying views of the port and Sea of Cortez. Browse around stalls selling handcrafted jewelry, pottery, woodcarvings, and artwork created by local artisans, and find unique souvenirs and presents to take home. Relax at waterfront cafes and restaurants nearby while viewing the gorgeous surroundings.

5. **Loreto Bay Farmers Market:** Visit the Loreto Bay Farmers Market, a weekly market hosted in the Loreto Bay community, where you can buy locally grown produce, organic foods, artisanal products, and homemade goods. Browse among stalls selling fresh fruits, vegetables, herbs, honey, baked goods, and gourmet snacks, and meet local farmers, craftsmen, and food producers who demonstrate their products. Enjoy live music, food demonstrations, and community events while supporting sustainable agriculture and small-scale producers.

6. **Tiendas de Artesanías (Craft Shops) in Downtown Loreto:** Explore the picturesque streets of downtown Loreto and discover a range of tiendas de artesanías (craft shops) offering a selection of handmade crafts, artwork, and souvenirs. Browse through shops selling hand-painted ceramics, embroidered fabrics, woven baskets, and indigenous crafts, and find unique pieces to enhance your home or wardrobe. Chat with store owners and learn about the cultural significance and craftsmanship behind each object while enjoying a leisurely stroll across town.

7. **La Tienda de Artesanías (The Artisan Shop) at Loreto Bay Resort:** Visit La Tienda de Artesanías (The Artisan Shop) located at Loreto Bay Resort, where you may shop for a selected variety of artisan crafts, jewelry,

clothes, and souvenirs manufactured by local craftsmen and designers. Browse through displays of handcrafted goods, unique gifts, and special items inspired by the natural beauty and cultural heritage of Loreto, and uncover things to keep as mementos of your visit to this lovely place.

## Handcrafted Goods and Artisanal Products

Discover the rich craftsmanship and artistic traditions of Loreto by exploring its handcrafted goods and artisanal products, which reflect the region's cultural heritage and natural beauty. Here are some places where you can find exquisite handcrafted items and unique artisanal products in Loreto:

1. **Artisan Markets and Tiendas de Artesanías (Craft Shops):** Explore the vibrant artisan markets and tiendas de artesanías (craft shops) scattered throughout Loreto, where you can find a diverse selection of handcrafted goods made by local artisans. Browse through stalls and shops selling handmade textiles, ceramics, pottery, woodcarvings, jewelry, and artwork inspired by the traditions and landscapes of Baja California Sur. Chat with artisans and learn about their craft techniques and

cultural influences while selecting one-of-a-kind treasures to take home as souvenirs or gifts.

2. **Mercado Municipal de Loreto (Loreto Municipal Market):** Visit the Mercado Municipal de Loreto, Loreto's main market, where you can shop for fresh produce, seafood, meats, spices, and a variety of artisanal products made by local vendors. Explore the market's bustling stalls and discover handmade crafts, woven baskets, embroidered textiles, and other artisanal goods alongside everyday essentials. Interact with vendors and artisans, and immerse yourself in the vibrant sights, sounds, and flavors of this lively marketplace.

3. **Marina Mercado Artesanal (Marina Artisan Market):** Experience the Marina Mercado Artesanal, a waterfront market located near the Loreto Marina, where you can find a selection of artisan crafts, gifts, and souvenirs made by local artisans. Browse through stalls selling handmade jewelry, pottery, leather goods, artwork, and decorative items, and admire the creativity and craftsmanship behind each piece. Enjoy views of the harbor and Sea of Cortez while shopping for unique treasures to commemorate your visit to Loreto.

4. **Artisan Workshops and Studios:** Take a behind-the-scenes look at the creative process by visiting artisan workshops and studios in Loreto, where you can

observe artisans at work and learn about traditional craft techniques firsthand. Explore workshops specializing in pottery, ceramics, weaving, woodcarving, and other artisanal skills, and see how raw materials are transformed into beautiful handmade goods. Participate in hands-on workshops or demonstrations to create your own masterpiece under the guidance of skilled artisans.

5. **Cultural Centers and Community Spaces:** Discover the cultural richness of Loreto by visiting cultural centers and community spaces that showcase local artwork, craftsmanship, and creative expression. Explore exhibitions, galleries, and art installations featuring works by local artists and artisans, and gain insight into the cultural heritage and artistic traditions of Baja California Sur. Attend cultural events, workshops, and performances to immerse yourself in the vibrant arts scene of Loreto and support the local creative community.

6. **Eco-Friendly and Sustainable Products:** Support environmentally conscious artisans and producers by seeking out eco-friendly and sustainable products made with natural materials and traditional techniques. Look for handmade goods crafted from recycled materials, organic fibers, and locally sourced ingredients, such as natural soaps, candles, textiles, and skincare products. Purchase eco-friendly souvenirs and gifts that promote

sustainability and responsible consumption, and contribute to the preservation of Loreto's natural environment and cultural heritage.

7. **Boutique Hotels and Resorts**: Explore boutique hotels and resorts in Loreto that showcase artisanal craftsmanship and locally made products in their design, decor, and amenities. Stay at properties that feature handcrafted furniture, artwork, textiles, and decor sourced from local artisans and craftsmen, and experience the authentic charm and character of Baja California Sur. Shop for unique souvenirs and gifts at hotel boutiques and artisan shops, and support sustainable tourism initiatives that promote cultural preservation and economic development.

These artisanal experiences offer a glimpse into the vibrant arts scene and creative spirit of Loreto, Mexico.

## Sustainable Shopping Options

Support sustainable shopping alternatives in Loreto by buying businesses and vendors who value environmental conservation, ethical practices, and community development. Here are some methods to buy sustainably in Loreto:

1. **Eco-Friendly Products:** Look for eco-friendly products manufactured from sustainable materials and techniques, such as organic textiles, natural skincare products, biodegradable home items, and recycled goods. Seek out stores and sellers who stress eco-friendly sourcing, packaging, and production processes to minimize environmental effect and promote responsible consumption.

2. **Locally Made items:** Support local artisans and craftsmen by purchasing handcrafted items and artisanal products manufactured in Loreto and the surrounding region. Shop for locally manufactured textiles, ceramics, jewelry, artwork, and souvenirs that display traditional skills and cultural history while helping to the local economy and community development.

3. **Fair Trade Certification:** Choose fair trade-certified products that assure fair salaries, safe working conditions, and sustainable livelihoods for producers and craftspeople. Look for fair trade labels and certifications on commodities such as coffee, chocolate, handicrafts, and textiles, showing ethical sourcing and support for underprivileged groups and small-scale producers.

4. **Sustainable Fashion:** Opt for sustainable fashion options, such as apparel, accessories, and footwear

manufactured from organic, recycled, or eco-friendly materials. Seek out businesses and designers committed to ethical manufacturing processes, transparency, and environmental stewardship, and favour quality, longevity, and timeless style over fast fashion trends.

5. **Farmers Markets and Local Producers:** Shop at farmers markets and support local producers, growers, and artisans that offer fresh, seasonal produce, organic foods, handmade crafts, and artisanal products. Purchase locally farmed fruits, vegetables, herbs, and artisanal goods, and lower the carbon footprint associated with long-distance transportation and distribution.

6. **Upcycled and Recycled Products:** Look for upcycled and repurposed products that offer new life to materials and resources, eliminating waste and promoting circular economy concepts. Choose things manufactured from salvaged or repurposed materials, such as furniture, home decor, accessories, and artwork, and support organisations that promote resource conservation and creative reuse.

7. **Community-Supported activities:** Get active in community-supported activities that promote sustainability, conservation, and social responsibility in Loreto. Participate in neighbourhood clean-up initiatives, conservation projects, and community gardens, and

support organizations and nonprofits striving to conserve the environment, preserve cultural heritage, and empower underprivileged people.

8. **Conscious Consumerism:** Practice conscious consumerism by making educated decisions and considering the environmental, social, and ethical ramifications of your purchases. Prioritize products and companies that connect with your beliefs and support sustainable practices, and push for positive change within the local community and marketplace.

By shopping responsibly in Loreto, you can make a good influence on the environment, assist local people, and contribute to the preservation of natural resources and cultural legacy. There are lots of possibilities to buy wisely and ethically while enjoying the beauty and charm of Loreto, Mexico.

# Chapter 9: Practical Information

## Currency and Payment Methods

When traveling to Loreto, it's crucial to educate yourself with the local currency and payment methods to guarantee seamless transactions during your vacation. Here's everything you need to know about currencies and payment choices in Loreto:

### Currency:

The official currency of Mexico is the Mexican Peso (MXN). Peso banknotes come in quantities of 20, 50, 100, 200, 500, and 1000 pesos, while coins are available in denominations of 1, 2, 5, 10, and 20 pesos, as well as smaller denominations known as centavos (cents).

### Accepted Payment Methods:

- *Cash:* Cash is readily accepted in Loreto for most transactions, including purchases at restaurants, shops, markets, and small enterprises. It's

suggested to carry small denominations of pesos for convenience and to avoid complications with making change.
- *Credit and Debit Cards:* Major credit and debit cards, such as Visa, Mastercard, and American Express, are routinely accepted at hotels, upscale restaurants, larger merchants, and tourist-oriented businesses in Loreto. However, it's always a good idea to have cash as a backup, especially when visiting more distant places or smaller establishments where card acceptance may be limited.
- *ATMs:* ATMs (cajeros automáticos) are accessible in Loreto, allowing you to withdraw Mexican pesos using your international debit or credit card. Look for ATMs linked with large banks for the best exchange rates and withdrawal alternatives. Keep in mind that some ATMs may impose additional fees for withdrawals, so check with your bank for details on foreign transaction fees and currency conversion charges.
- *Traveler's Checks:* While traveler's checks were formerly a popular form of payment for overseas travel, they are less often used today due to the widespread availability of ATMs and the convenience of credit and debit cards. However, if you prefer to utilize traveler's checks, you can exchange them for Mexican pesos at banks or

currency exchange offices in Loreto, although fees and conversion rates may apply.
- *Mobile Payment programmes:* Mobile payment programmes such as Apple Pay and Google Pay are not extensively utilised in Loreto, so it's better to rely on cash or card payments for most transactions.

## Currency Exchange:

Currency exchange services are provided in banks, exchange offices (casas de cambio), and some hotels in Loreto. While it's convenient to exchange cash at the airport upon arrival, rates may be less favorable compared to those given at banks or exchange offices in town. Be sure to compare exchange rates and fees before exchanging money to receive the most value for your currency.

## Tips for Handling Money:

- Keep your cash, credit cards, and critical papers secure at all times, especially in crowded or touristy places where pickpocketing may occur.
- Inform your bank of your travel plans in advance to prevent your cards from being stopped or flagged for suspicious behaviour while overseas.

- Carry a combination of cash and cards for flexibility, and store emergency funds in a separate, secure location such as a money belt or secret pocket.
- Familiarize yourself with currency conversion rates to avoid overpaying for goods and services, and be cautious while exchanging money with individuals on the street.

By understanding the currency and payment alternatives accessible in Loreto, you may comfortably handle financial transactions throughout your visit and enjoy a hassle-free vacation experience in this wonderful destination.

## Language Spoken in Loreto

The major language spoken in Loreto, Mexico, is Spanish. As in most of Mexico, Spanish serves as the official language and is extensively spoken by the local populace. Visitors to Loreto will find that Spanish is used in everyday communication, including interactions with inhabitants, businesses, and government institutions.

While Spanish is the major language, you may also encounter some English speakers in tourist districts, hotels, restaurants, and stores catering to international visitors. However, outside of these tourist-oriented establishments, competency in English may vary among the local people.

Learning some simple Spanish phrases and greetings will enrich your trip experience and facilitate conversation with locals. Additionally, taking a pocket-sized Spanish phrasebook or using translation apps on your smartphone might be helpful for navigating frequent scenarios and communicating with Spanish-speaking individuals.

While Spanish is the primary language in Loreto, visitors from English-speaking nations can still enjoy their time in the city with a willingness to interact and engage with the local culture and community.

## Emergency Contact Numbers

When traveling to Loreto, Mexico, it's necessary to be prepared for any emergency scenarios that may develop. Here are some crucial emergency contact numbers to keep handy during your trip:

1. **Emergency Services:** For emergencies needing police, medical, or fire help, dial *911* from any phone. This number connects you to the relevant emergency services, and operators are often bilingual in Spanish and English.

2. **Tourist Assistance Hotline:** For non-emergency assistance and information connected to tourism, safety, and travel in Loreto, you can contact the Tourist Assistance Hotline at *078*. This hotline is administered by the Secretary of Tourism and provides support and guidance to travelers.

3. **Medical Emergencies:** In the event of a medical emergency, you can contact local hospitals, clinics, or medical institutions for assistance. Here are some essential medical contacts in Loreto:
   - Hospital Salvatierra: *+52 613 135 1077*
   - Red Cross (Cruz Roja Mexicana): *+52 613 135 2121*

4. **Consular Aid:** If you are a foreign traveler in need of consular aid or support from your country's embassy or consulate, call the nearest consulate or embassy. Here are the contact details for some consulates in Mexico:
   - United States Embassy in Mexico City: *+52 55 5080 2000*

- Canadian Embassy in Mexico City: *+52 55 5724 7900*
- British Embassy in Mexico City: *+52 55 1670 3200*

5. **Roadside Assistance**: In case of a roadside emergency or vehicle breakdown, you can contact your rental car company or insurance provider for assistance. Additionally, the Green Angels (Angeles Verdes) give free roadside assistance to travelers on Mexican roadways. Dial 078 or look for their green trucks for aid.

6. **Local Authorities:** For non-emergency issues requiring assistance from local authorities, you can contact the Loreto Municipal Police at their non-emergency number: *+52 613 135 2115*.

7. **Coast Guard (Maritime Emergencies):** In case of maritime emergencies or water-related incidents, you can contact the Mexican Coast Guard (Secretaría de Marina) for assistance. Their emergency hotline is 911.

It's important to save these emergency contact numbers in your phone and maintain a written copy in your travel documents or lodging. Being prepared and knowing who to contact in case of an emergency will assist secure your safety and well-being during your stay to Loreto, Mexico.

# Chapter 10: Responsible Travel Practices

## Environmental Conservation Efforts

Environmental conservation initiatives play a critical role in conserving the natural beauty and biodiversity of Loreto, Mexico, a region recognised for its breathtaking landscapes, rich marine life, and various ecosystems. Here are some important activities and organizations dedicated to environmental conservation in Loreto:

1. **Loreto Bay National Marine Park:** Established in 1996, the Loreto Bay National Marine Park is a protected region comprising about 2,000 square kilometers of marine and coastal habitats, including islands, reefs, mangroves, and seagrass beds. The park is home to a vast range of marine creatures, including whales, dolphins, sea turtles, and countless fish and invertebrate species. Conservation initiatives inside the maritime park focus on habitat protection, sustainable fishing methods, and marine biodiversity monitoring to preserve the long-term health and resilience of the ecosystem.

2. **Eco-Awareness Programs:** Local organizations and environmental groups in Loreto perform eco-awareness activities and educational projects to encourage environmental stewardship and create knowledge about conservation concerns. These programs frequently target schools, community groups, and tourists, delivering knowledge on themes such as marine conservation, waste management, sustainable tourism practices, and the necessity of safeguarding natural resources.

3. **Marine Mammal Research and Conservation:** Loreto is a hotspot for marine mammal research and conservation efforts, with organizations such as the Gulf of California Marine Program (Programa Marino del Golfo de California) conducting scientific studies and conservation projects focused on species such as blue whales, fin whales, humpback whales, and dolphins. Research activities try to study population dynamics, behavior, and habitat usage, while conservation projects work to alleviate concerns such as habitat degradation, pollution, and human disturbance.

4. **Sustainable Tourism Practices:** The tourism industry in Loreto plays a vital role in encouraging environmental conservation through sustainable tourism practices and responsible travel programmes. Tour operators, hotels, and eco-lodges often implement measures to minimize their environmental footprint, such as reducing energy

and water consumption, managing waste responsibly, supporting local conservation projects, and offering educational programs that promote eco-friendly behavior among visitors.

5. **Community-Based Conservation Projects:** Community-based conservation projects engage local residents in conservation activities and enable them to become stewards of their natural environment. These programmes frequently involve collaboration between local people, government agencies, NGOs, and researchers to address conservation concerns, safeguard natural resources, and promote sustainable lives. Examples of community-based activities in Loreto include mangrove restoration projects, marine trash cleanup efforts, and sustainable fisheries management programs.

6. **Protected Areas and Biosphere Reserves:** Loreto is home to various protected areas and biosphere reserves established to conserve its unique ecosystems and wildlife. These include the Loreto Bay National Marine Park, the Islands of the Gulf of California Biosphere Reserve, and the Sierra de la Giganta Biosphere Reserve. These protected areas provide home for endangered species, safeguard valuable natural resources, and give possibilities for scientific research, recreation, and eco-tourism.

7. **Conservation Partnerships and Collaborations:** Collaboration between government agencies, non-profit organizations, academia, and local communities is vital for effective conservation in Loreto. Partnerships such as the Gulf of California Conservation Fund (Fondo Mexicano para la Conservación de la Naturaleza) bring together stakeholders to promote conservation projects, fund research initiatives, and adopt sustainable management practices that benefit both people and the environment.

Support these environmental conservation efforts and adopt sustainable practices. Loreto can continue to grow as a destination while protecting its natural heritage for future generations to enjoy. Visitors can contribute to conservation by choosing eco-friendly activities, respecting wildlife and ecosystems, and supporting businesses and projects that prioritize environmental protection and sustainability.

# Respectful Interaction with Local Culture

Respectful connection with the local culture is crucial when visiting Loreto, Mexico, as it builds healthy relationships, increases cultural understanding, and assures a memorable travel experience for both visitors and residents. Here are some guidelines for appropriately connecting with the local culture in Loreto:

1. **Learn Basic Spanish Phrases:** While English may be spoken in tourist areas, making an effort to learn simple Spanish phrases such as hello, please, thank you, and excuse me can go a long way in expressing respect for the local language and culture. Locals enjoy guests who endeavour to speak in Spanish, even if it's just a few words.

2. **Respect Cultural Norms and Customs:** Take the time to learn about the cultural norms, practices, and traditions of Loreto, and observe local etiquette when engaging with inhabitants. Pay attention to social cues, such as greetings, gestures, and demonstrations of respect, and follow the lead of locals in social situations.

3. **Dress Respectfully:** Dress modestly and appropriately when visiting cultural sites, religious sites, and local communities out of respect for the local customs and traditions. Avoid wearing revealing apparel or unpleasant attire, especially in holy or conservative contexts.

4. **Ask Permission Before Taking images**: Always ask for permission before taking images of individuals,

especially portraits or close-ups. Respect individuals' privacy and cultural beliefs, and refrain from photographing holy ceremonies, rituals, or sacred sites without permission.

5. **Support Local Businesses and Artisans:** Support the local economy and artisans by purchasing handcrafted crafts, souvenirs, and products manufactured by local artisans and businesses. Seek out real experiences, such as dining at family-owned restaurants, shopping at markets, and participating in cultural activities that support the livelihoods of local communities.

6. **Practice Responsible Tourism:** Be careful of your environmental effect and practice responsible tourism by limiting trash, conserving water and energy, and protecting natural habitats and wildlife. Follow authorised pathways, adhere to park rules and regulations, and leave no trace when exploring nature.

7. **Engage with Respect and Curiosity:** Approach encounters with locals with respect, curiosity, and an open mind. Listen intently, ask questions, and show real interest in learning about the local culture, history, and way of life. Be sensitive to diverse ideas and experiences, and avoid making assumptions or judgments based on cultural stereotypes.

8. **Express Gratitude and Appreciation:** Show thanks and admiration for the hospitality and compassion of locals by saying thank you (gracias) and expressing your appreciation for their assistance, recommendations, and insights. A genuine smile and a few words of gratitude can go a long way in developing strong connections and fostering goodwill.

By following these recommendations for respectful interaction with the local culture in Loreto, you can enrich your vacation experience, build important connections with locals, and contribute to a good exchange of cultural understanding and appreciation. Remember to approach each interaction with humility, empathy, and respect for the diversity and richness of the local community.

## Minimizing Your Ecological Footprint

Minimizing your ecological footprint is vital for responsible tourism in Loreto, Mexico, as it helps maintain the region's natural ecosystem, minimise carbon emissions, and preserve its biodiversity for future generations to enjoy. Here are some recommendations for minimizing your ecological footprint while visiting Loreto:

1. **Choose Eco-Friendly Accommodations:** Stay in eco-friendly hotels, resorts, or lodges that stress sustainable practices such as energy and water conservation, waste reduction, and environmental stewardship. Look for certifications such as LEED (Leadership in Energy and Environmental Design) or eco-labels showing green activities.

2. **Conserve Water and Energy:** Practice water and energy conservation by taking shorter showers, shutting off lights and air conditioning when not in use, and using reusable towels and sheets. Be careful of your energy consumption and use energy-efficient equipment and lighting whenever available.

3. **Reduce, Reuse, Recycle:** Reduce waste by minimizing single-use plastics and disposable products such as water bottles, straws, and plastic bags. Bring a reusable water bottle, shopping bag, and reusable utensils to decrease waste and prevent contributing to plastic pollution. Dispose of garbage responsibly by recycling and properly disposing of trash in designated bins.

4. **Support Sustainable Transportation:** Choose sustainable transportation options such as walking, biking, or taking public transportation to explore Loreto and lessen your carbon footprint. If renting a car, choose for fuel-efficient or electric vehicles, and carpool or use ridesharing services wherever possible to minimize emissions.

5. **Respect Wildlife and Natural Habitats:** Observe wildlife from a distance and avoid disturbing or feeding animals in their natural habitat. Respect protected areas, wildlife sanctuaries, and marine reserves by following park rules and regulations, staying on approved pathways, and avoiding vulnerable habitats such as coral reefs and nesting sites.

6. **Practice Responsible Marine Tourism:** When engaging in water-based activities such as snorkeling, diving, or kayaking, practice responsible marine tourism by respecting marine life, avoiding touching or harassing marine organisms, and using reef-safe sunscreen to protect coral reefs and marine ecosystems.

7. **Support Local Conservation Efforts:** Contribute to local conservation efforts by supporting organizations, non-profits, or community-based initiatives dedicated to protecting the environment, conserving natural resources, and promoting sustainable development in

Loreto. Consider offering your time or donating to conservation projects or environmental education programs.

8. **Educate Yourself and Others:** Educate yourself and others about the importance of environmental conservation and sustainable tourism practices. Share your knowledge and experiences with friends, family, and fellow travelers, and motivate others to adopt eco-friendly practices and make responsible decisions when traveling.

# Glossary of Loreto Related Terms

Here's a glossary of Loreto-related terminology to assist you better appreciate the area and its unique features:

1. **Loreto:** The name of the town and municipality located on the eastern coast of the Baja California Peninsula in Mexico.

2. **Baja California Peninsula:** A long peninsula in Northwestern Mexico, separating the Pacific Ocean from the Gulf of California (Sea of Cortez).

3. **Sea of Cortez:** Also known as the Gulf of California, it is a marginal sea of the Pacific Ocean, surrounded by the Baja California Peninsula and mainland Mexico.

4. **Marine Park**: A protected area intended to preserve and conserve marine ecosystems, including coral reefs, marine life, and coastal habitats.

5. **Marine Life:** Refers to the varied array of plant and animal species inhabiting marine settings, such as fish, marine mammals, sea turtles, and coral reefs.

6. **Islands of Loreto**: Refers to the islands located off the coast of Loreto, including Isla Coronado, Isla Carmen, and Isla Danzante, recognised for their scenic beauty, fauna, and recreational activities.

7. **Ecotourism:** Tourism focuses on experiencing and maintaining natural surroundings and promoting conservation initiatives, frequently includes activities such as wildlife watching, hiking, and snorkeling.

8. **Mangroves:** Coastal ecosystems consisting of salt-tolerant trees and shrubs, defined by their distinct root systems and biodiversity, providing habitat for diverse marine species and functioning as natural buffers against erosion and storms.

9. **Sierra de la Giganta**: A mountain range located near Loreto, famed for its difficult topography, magnificent vistas, and trekking opportunities.

10. **Whale Watching:** A popular activity in Loreto, allowing opportunity to watch whales, including blue whales, humpback whales, and gray whales, during their seasonal migrations.

11. **Sport Fishing:** Fishing for leisure purposes, frequently targeting game fish such as marlin, dorado,

tuna, and sailfish, popular among visitors to Loreto due to its vast fishing grounds.

12. **Kayaking:** The activity of paddling a kayak, a small watercraft, widely utilised for exploring coastal areas, sea caves, and marine reserves in Loreto.

13. **Snorkeling:** Undersea diving activity that involves swimming near the surface of the water with a snorkel mask and fins to see marine life and undersea scenery, popular in Loreto's beautiful, shallow waters.

14. **Scuba Diving:** Underwater diving activity that involves using a self-contained underwater breathing apparatus (SCUBA) to explore deeper underwater areas, including coral reefs, underwater caves, and shipwrecks.

15. **Eco-Lodges:** Accommodations that prioritize sustainability and eco-friendly operations, frequently located in natural surroundings and allowing visitors chances to engage in environmentally responsible activities and experiences.

16. **Desert Landscape:** Refers to the arid, desert topography characteristic of the Baja California Peninsula, with cacti, succulents, and distinctive flora and fauna suited to dry circumstances.

17. **Biosphere Reserves:** Designated regions of land and water managed for protection and sustainable use, recognized for their ecological value and biodiversity, such as the Islands of the Gulf of California Biosphere Reserve.

18. **Conservation**: The conservation, preservation, and sustainable management of natural resources, wildlife, and ecosystems, aimed at maintaining ecological balance and biodiversity.

19. **Sustainable Tourism:** Tourism that avoids negative effects on the environment, supports local people, and encourages conservation initiatives, contributing to the long-term sustainability of places like Loreto.

20. **Cultural Heritage:** Refers to the traditions, customs, beliefs, and artifacts passed down through generations, including indigenous cultures, historic locations, and cultural practices peculiar to Loreto and the surrounding region.

# Conclusion and Departure Tips

As your adventure through the stunning landscapes and rich cultural tapestry of Loreto, Mexico, draws to a conclusion, it's time to reflect on the remarkable experiences you've had and prepare for your departure. In this concluding piece, we give some departing recommendations and final thoughts to ensure a seamless and memorable end to your adventure:

## To End With

As you wave farewell to Loreto, take a moment to cherish the experiences you've made and the connections you've developed along the road. From the stunning sunsets over the Sea of Cortez to the wonderful welcome of the local community, Loreto has left an everlasting impact on your heart.

**Departure Tips:**

1. **Check Your Travel Documents:** Ensure that you have all appropriate travel documents, including your

passport, visa (if required), boarding passes, and any other applicable paperwork. Double-check flight details and transportation arrangements to the airport.

2. **Pack Wisely:** Organize your items and pack them securely, taking care to provide room for any souvenirs or gifts you've accumulated throughout your visit. Remember to take important goods such as prescriptions, chargers, and travel-sized toiletries in your carry-on luggage.

3. **Settle Outstanding Bills:** Settle any outstanding bills with your hotels, restaurants, or tour operators, then convert any remaining local cash for your home currency at a trustworthy exchange office.

4. **Say Goodbye to Loreto:** Take a final stroll along the waterfront promenade, take some last-minute shots of the gorgeous surroundings, and wave farewell to the quaint streets and colorful buildings of Loreto. Leave behind a bit of your heart as you remember the memories of your time at this magnificent destination.

5. **Convey Gratitude:** Take the time to convey your gratitude to the people, hotel staff, tour guides, and anyone else who has made your stay in Loreto unforgettable. A heartfelt thank-you goes a long way in

conveying appreciation for the hospitality and compassion you've received.

6. **Plan Your Return:** Though your time in Loreto may be coming to an end, let it be the beginning of a lifetime love affair with this lovely destination. Start dreaming of your future visit and begin planning your return to experience more of what Loreto has to offer.

As you prepare to depart from Loreto, bring with you the memories of its breathtaking landscapes, rich culture, and friendly hospitality. Though you may be departing for now, know that Loreto will always welcome you back with open arms whenever you're ready to return.

Until we meet again, may your travel be safe, your adventures be plentiful, and your heart eternally filled with the charm of Loreto, Mexico. ¡Hasta pronto! (Until next time!)

Made in the USA
Columbia, SC
31 January 2025